Josemaría Escrivá

THE WAY

SCEPTER
London New York

This edition is published:
in England by Scepter (U.K.) Ltd., 21 Hinton Avenue, Hounslow TW4 6AP; e-mail: scepter@pobox.com;
in the United States by Scepter Publishers Inc., P. O. Box 211, New York, NY 10018-0004; e-mail: info @scepterpublishers.org; www.scepterpublishers.org

With ecclesiastical approval
ISBN 9789061386636

Typeset by MI Intermedia, and printed in China.

CONTENTS

INTRODUCTION

These penetrating lines, these concise thoughts are addressed to you, dear reader. Ponder each word and steep yourself in its meaning.

The spirit of God hovers over these pages. Behind each maxim is a saint who sees your intention and waits for your decisions. The sentences are left broken, for you to round them off with your conduct.

Don't recoil: your life is going to be a soothing of suffering. This is why you are a disciple of the Master!

Your worst enemy is yourself, because your flesh is weak and earthly, but you have to be strong and heavenly. The centre of gravity of your body is the world; your centre of gravity must be heaven. Your heart is all God's and you have to consecrate its affections entirely to him.

Don't rest, dear reader. Always be watchful and alert, because the enemy does not sleep. If you turn these maxims into your own life, you will be a perfect imitator of Jesus Christ and a flawless gentleman. And with Christs like you, Spain will return to the old grandeur of her saints, scholars and heroes.

+ Xavier
Apostolic Administrator of Vitoria
Vitoria, Feast of St Joseph, 1939.

THE AUTHOR

St Josemaría Escrivá de Balaguer was born in Barbastro, in northern Spain, on 9 January 1902. At the age of 15 or 16 he began to feel the first intimations that God was calling him and he decided to become a priest. He started his ecclesiastical studies in the Seminary of Logroño in 1918, and later, in 1920, in that of St Francis de Paula in Saragossa, where from 1922 he was a superior or tutor. In 1923 he began to study Civil Law in the University of Saragossa, with the permission of his ecclesiastical superiors. These studies did not interfere with his theological studies. He was ordained deacon on 20 December 1924 and became a priest on 28 March 1925.

He began his work as a priest in the village of Perdiguera, within the diocese of Saragossa, and afterwards in Saragossa itself. In the spring of 1927, with the permission of the Archbishop of Saragossa, he moved to the Spanish capital, Madrid, and there carried out abundant priestly work among all kinds of people, devoting attention also to the poor and destitute in the outlying districts of the city, and especially to the incurably sick and the dying in the hospitals. He worked as chaplain to the *Patronato de Enfermos* (Foundation for the Sick), a welfare organisation run by the Apostolic Sisters of the Sacred Heart. He also taught at a university academy, and continued his studies for a doctorate in Civil Law, which at that time could only be obtained from the University of Madrid.

On 2 October 1928 God made him *see* clearly what up to then he had only had inklings of; and St Josemaría Escrivá founded Opus Dei (in English, the Work of God). Under God's continuing guidance, on 14 February 1930 he understood that he must open up the apostolic work of Opus Dei to women also. As a result, a new path was opening up in the Church, to promote, among people of all social classes, the search for holiness and the practice of the apostolate, through the sanctification of ordinary work, in the midst of the world and without changing one's state in life.

From 2 October 1928, the Founder of Opus Dei directed his energies to the mission God had entrusted to him, with great apostolic zeal for all souls. In 1934 he was appointed Rector of the *Patronato de Santa Isabel* (St Elizabeth Foundation). During the Spanish Civil War, at times putting his life at risk, he carried out his priestly ministry in Madrid and, subsequently, in the northern city of Burgos. Already in those years St Josemaría Escrivá experienced harsh and sustained opposition, which he bore calmly and with a supernatural outlook.

On 14 February 1943 he founded the Priestly Society of the Holy Cross, which is inseparably united to Opus Dei and which, as well as opening up the possibility of ordaining lay members of Opus Dei to the priesthood and incardinating them for the service of the Work, would later on also enable priests who are incardinated in dioceses to share the spirituality and asceticism of Opus Dei, seeking holiness in the exercise of their ministerial duties, while remaining exclusively under their respective Ordinaries.

In 1946 he took up residence in Rome, which was to be his home for the rest of his life. From there, he stimulated and guided the development of Opus Dei throughout the world, using all his energies to give to the men and women of Opus Dei a solid formation in doctrine, ascetical spirit and apostolate. At the time of his death, Opus Dei had more than 60,000 members from 80 different nationalities.

St Josemaría was a Consultor to the Pontifical Commission for the authentic interpretation of the Code of Canon Law, and to the Sacred Congregation for Seminaries and Universities. He was a Domestic Prelate and an honorary Academician of the Pontifical Roman Academy of Theology. He was also the Chancellor of the Universities of Navarre (in Spain) and Piura (in Peru).

St Josemaría died on 26 June 1975. For years, he had been offering his life for the Church and for the Pope. He was buried in the Crypt of the church of Our Lady of

Peace, in Rome. Bishop Alvaro del Portillo (1914-1994), who for many years had been his closest collaborator, was unanimously elected to succeed him. The present Prelate of Opus Dei is Bishop Javier Echevarría, who also worked for several decades with St Josemaría Escrivá and with his first successor, Bishop del Portillo. Opus Dei, which from its inception had had the approval of the diocesan authorities and, from 1943, also the *appositio manuum* and subsequently the approval of the Holy See, was established as a Personal Prelature by His Holiness Pope John Paul II on 28 November 1982: this was the canonical formula foreseen and desired by St Josemaría Escrivá.

The reputation for holiness which the Founder of Opus Dei enjoyed in his lifetime has spread after his death to the far corners of the earth, as can be seen from countless spiritual and material favours attributed to his intercession; among them, a number of cures which are medically inexplicable. Many letters from all the continents, and among them those of 69 Cardinals and nearly 1,300 Bishops (more than a third of the episcopate worldwide), were written requesting the Pope to open the Causc of Beatification and Canonisation of St Josemaría. The Congregation for the Causes of Saints gave its *nihil obstat* for the opening of the Cause on 30 January 1981 and this was ratified by Pope John Paul II on 5 February 1981.

Between 1981 and 1986 two processes took place, one in Rome and the other in Madrid, to gather information on the life and virtues of Msgr. Escrivá. Following the results of these two processes and accepting the favourable opinions of the congress of theological consultors and the Commission of Cardinals and Bishops members of the Congregation for the Causes of Saints, the Holy Father on 9 April 1990 declared the heroicity of the virtues of Msgr. Escrivá, who thus received the title of Venerable. On 6 July 1991 the Pope commanded the publication of a Decree declaring the miraculous nature of a cure attributed to the intercession of the Venerable Josemaría Escrivá. This act completed the juridical stages for the beatification of the Founder of Opus Dei, which was celebrated in Rome on 17 May 1992, in a solemn ceremony presided over by His Holiness Pope John Paul II in St Peter's Square. From 21 May 1992 the body of St Josemaría rests beneath the altar of the prelatic church of Our Lady of Peace, in the central offices of the Prelature of Opus Dei. It is accompanied constantly by the prayers and thanksgiving of many people from all over the world who have been brought closer to God, attracted by the example and teachings of the Founder of Opus Dei and by the devotion of those who turn to his intercession. Josemaría Escrivá was canonised in Rome on 6 October 2002.

Among his published writings, apart from the theological and legal study *La Abadesa de la Huelgas*, there are books of spirituality which have been translated into numerous languages: *The Way, Holy Rosary, Christ is passing by, Friends of God, The Way of the Cross, In Love with the Church, Furrow,* and *The Forge* (the last five titles have been published posthumously). Another book, which brings together press interviews, has the title *Conversations with Msgr. Escrivá de Balaguer*.

PREFACE

'They are things I whisper in your ear, confiding in you as a friend, a brother, a father ... so that some thought may come to you that will strike you: and that way you will improve your life and enter upon ways of prayer and of Love.' With these words the author begins a book whose purpose is to show men and women how to live in contact with God their Father day after day.

The Way was first published in 1934 under the title *Consideraciones espirituales* and in 1939, when the second, longer text appeared, it was given its definitive Spanish title, *Camino*. Since then millions of people, of very varied races, cultures and walks of life, have found in these words of Monsignor Escrivá light and strength to help them recognise God and give meaning to their lives. The growth in the number of editions of the book in many languages – its circulation is now measured in millions of copies – is one of the clearest signs of how it has been received. In a very short time *The Way* has become a classic of spiritual literature, an 'à Kempis for modern times' as some have described it.

This preface, then, is designed not so much to present the book as to suggest the reasons for its success.

'*The Way* shows the eternal character of the Church and at the same time its inexhaustible capacity for renewal': this was how a French journalist summed up the impression the book had made on him *(Le Figaro,* 24 March 1964). This is in fact the main quality of *The Way:* the depth and vitality of its message, announcing as it does that the word of Christ is not something dead but a living reality capable of changing the life of every man who does not close his heart to it. *The Way* encourages the reader to confront himself with the Gospel and so relive Christ's life: 'I don't understand how you can call yourself a

Christian and lead such an aimless, useless life. –Have you forgotten Christ's life of toil? (*The Way,* 356); 'Would that your bearing and conversation were such that everyone who sees you or hears you speak could say: This man reads the life of Jesus Christ.' (2)

The Christian should, 'following in the footsteps of the Master' (213), accept in a responsible way the mission which baptism confers on him: "'Go, preach the Gospel... I will be with you...' –Jesus has said this... and he has said it to you." (904)

The author of *The Way* shows that this invitation or calling does not, in itself, involve an invitation to leave one's place, to choose another way of life; in fact, for the great majority of Christians it is an invitation to face the ordinary circumstances of one's existence and find there a divine way which must be made holy. That is why Monsignor Escrivá rejects the temptation to 'get out of place' (832) because this amounts to avoiding the will of God. Each Christian must find a holiness in keeping with his own mission and his own state-in-life; and so the ordinary Christian, who lives in the middle of the secular world, should sanctify himself and others by means of the world itself, sanctifying his daily work and his whole life.

Human existence is thus set in a framework of faith, hope and love. The reader grows in awareness of God's presence and learns to listen to his voice which speaks through the people and happenings of daily life. 'We live as though the Lord were far away, in the starlit heavens, and we don't consider that he is also always by our side... We need to be imbued, to be saturated with the knowledge that the Lord, who is close beside us and in heaven, is our Father and very much our Father.' (267) 'You have told me sometimes that you are like a badly adjusted clock, which strikes at the wrong time: you are cold, dry and arid at the time of your prayer; and, on the other hand, when it is least to be expected, in the street, in your daily activities, in the midst of the bustle and hubbub of the city, or in the concentrated calm of your professional work, you find yourself praying... At the wrong time? Possibly; but don't let those chimes of your clock go to waste. –The spirit breathes where it will.' (110) 'Get to know the Holy Spirit – the Great Unknown – for it is he who is to sanctify you. Don't forget that you are God's temple. –The Paraclete is in the centre of your soul: listen to him and be docile to his inspirations.' (57)

This supernatural message, this telling of God, is not given in *The Way* as a hollow exhortation but as an expression of an intensely vital life: these pages reflect Monsignor Escrivá's work as a priest, which began in 1925. The book is in fact made up of passages from sacred Scripture, snatches of conversation, personal experiences, fragments of letters. In May 1933, for example, the author gave a young architectural student a present of a *Life of Christ* on which he wrote a few words as a dedication, and that was the origin of point 382: 'When I made you a present of that Life of Jesus, I wrote in it this inscription: "May you seek Christ: May you find Christ: May you love Christ. –They are three perfectly clear stages. Have you tried, at least, to live the first?'

This is one of the main attractions of the

book – its direct, conversational style, its personal and deeply human character. As a reviewer in *L'Osservatore Romano* (24 March 1950) put it: 'Monsignor Escrivá has written something more than a masterpiece; he has written straight from the heart, and straight to the heart go the short paragraphs which make up *The Way.*'

This deeply felt humanity is not an accidental characteristic of the book: it is in fact part of the very essence of the spirit which pervades it. Monsignor Escrivá's central theme is precisely the statement that the human is not foreign to the divine: it is not a part of man but the whole man who is loved and called by God, and therefore the fully Christian spiritual attitude can be described as 'unity of life.'

The above paragraphs have touched on some of the basic characteristics of the book and should help one to understand its lasting value. But these remarks would be incomplete if mention were not made of the historical importance of the book and the mark it has made on the history of the Church.

Since 1928 Monsignor Escrivá's

pastoral work has found concrete expression in the founding of Opus Dei, that is to say in the task of opening up a way of lay holiness in the middle of the world. Thus, *The Way* is intimately bound up with the history of the founding of Opus Dei although it is not an exposition of its spirit nor is it addressed only to its members: it is an invitation to all men of good will to share in the 'craziness' of following Christ (916).

During the years when the book was being written, Monsignor Escrivá mixed for the most part with workers and with students at Madrid University. It was to these students that he specially dedicated *Consideraciones espirituales* which, he tells us in the Introduction, were written in response to the spiritual needs of young university men and women to whom he gave guidance.

This fact does give us the historical context of quite a few points of *The Way,* but above all it emphasises one of the basic traits of the book: the fact that it was written with eyes on the world, looking at men and women who want to sanctify themselves in their earthly interests and activities, and proposing a teaching which can be applied to any type of age, circumstance or work: 'What amazes you seems reasonable enough to me. –So God has sought you out in the practice of your profession? That's how he sought the first, Peter, Andrew, John and James, by their nets; Matthew, sitting at his tax-collector's bench...' (799) 'You have an obligation to sanctify yourself. –Yes, you too. –Who thinks that this task is only for priests and religious? To everyone, without exception, Our Lord said: "Be perfect, as my Heavenly Father is perfect."' (291)

At the time when *The Way* first appeared, preaching like this was not merely unexpected – it was revolutionary. Among some people – who seemed to have lost touch with the renewing spirit of the Gospel – it provoked surprise and misunderstanding; for very many more this very surprise was turned into joy: for them the words of *The Way* were a revelation which made them more aware of their dignity as Christians and of the divine mission which, as Christians, they had in the world. *The Way* led many people to live what some years later the Church solemnly proclaimed in Vatican II: 'In the Church not everyone marches along the same path, yet all are called to holiness and have obtained an equal privilege of faith through the justice of God (cf. 2 Peter 1:1). There is a true equality between all with regard to the dignity and to the activity which is common to all the faithful in the building up of the Body of Christ' (Dogm. Const. *Lumen gentium,* 32).

Monsignor Escrivá's work has left its mark on the features of contemporary Christianity and this book, which embodies crucial moments in his life, is part of that work.

Born out of a deep Christian experience, *The Way* aims at encouraging people to love God and live by God. For this reason it assumes on the reader's part a desire for the divine. Anyone who reads these pages with any other intention would only distort their meaning by approaching them from a standpoint foreign to the spirit and intention of the author. To benefit from reading *The Way* one must have a minimum of faith in the capacity of men to recognise the life of the spirit.

'I am the light of the world; anyone who follows me will not be walking in the dark; he will have the light of life' (John 8:12). The 999 points which make up *The Way* were written in a desire to help us to see this light, so that all the ways of the earth, the ordinary ways of all men, might be ways of holiness open to the hope of the Kingdom which 'is not of this world' (John 18:36). Anyone who reads with this same desire will not have opened this book in vain.

EDITIONS OF *THE WAY*

To date *The Way* has appeared with a total printing of close to five million copies in 49 languages: Albanian, Amharic (Ethiopia), Arabic, Armenian (Eastern and Western), Basque, Bulgarian, Burmese, Catalan, Chinese, Croatian, Czech, Danish, Dutch, English, Esperanto, Estonian, Finnish, French, Galician, German, Greek, Guarani, Hebrew, Hiligaynon, Hungarian, Indonesian, Irish, Italian, Japanese, Korean, Latvian, Lithuanian, Maltese, Malayalam, Polish, Portuguese, Quechua, Romanian, Russian, Slovak, Slovenian, Spanish, Swahili, Swedish, Tagalog, Tigrinya (Eritrea), Ukrainian and Vietnamese.

There are also editions in Braille in English, German, Portuguese and Spanish.

Translations into the following languages are in preparation at present: Cebuan, Latin, Norwegian and Tamil.

Note to the Third Edition

Within a few months, the first edition of this book had run out, and the second edition suffered the same fate. The Portuguese edition is now with the printers, and from Rome there are requests to bring out a version in Italian soon.

We have refreshing reports – letters from priests, from religious and above all from young people – about the supernatural fruit that these pages have yielded in many souls. May the constant reading of this book, my friend, help you to straighten out and consolidate your 'way'.

This is the request to the Lord for you, from

The Author

Segovia, on the Feast of the Exaltation of the Holy Cross, 14 September 1945.

Note to the Seventh Edition

I have been asked to preface some words to the seventh edition of *The Way*.

The only thing that occurs to me to say to you, dear reader, is that you place this book in the hands of many, so that our divine madness of having a close relationship with Christ will take hold of many hearts; and that you pray, to our Lord and to his blessed Mother, for me, so that you and I will meet again soon in another book of mine – *Furrow* – which I intend to give you in a few months.

The Author

Rome, on the Feast of the Immaculate Conception, December of the Holy Year of 1950.

FOREWORD

Read these counsels slowly.
Meditate on these considerations, pausing over them.
They are things that I whisper in your ear,
confiding in you as a friend, a brother,
a father.
And our confidential conversation is being listened to by God.
I won't be telling you anything new:
I am going to stir your memories,
so that some thought may come to you
that will strike you:
and that way you will improve your life
and enter upon ways of prayer
and of Love.
And end up becoming a soul of worth.

CHARACTER

1 Don't let your life be barren. –Be useful. –Leave a mark. –Shine forth, with the torch of your faith and your love.

Wipe out, with your apostolic life, the filthy, viscous trail left by the impure sowers of hatred. –And set aflame all the ways of the earth with the fire of Christ that you bear in your heart.

2 Would that your bearing and conversation were such that everyone who sees you or hears you speak could say: This man reads the life of Jesus Christ.

3 Gravity. –Stop behaving like a giddy woman or a foolish child. –Let your outward conduct reflect the peace and order of

your soul.

4 Don't say: "It's the way I'm made..., it's my character." It's your lack of character: Be a man – *Esto vir*.

5 Get used to saying No.

6 Turn your back on the villain when he whispers in your ear: "Why complicate your life?"

7 Don't have a small-town outlook. –Enlarge your heart till it becomes universal, "catholic".

Don't flutter about like a farmyard fowl, when you can soar like the eagles.

8 Serenity. –Why lose your temper if by doing so you offend God, annoy your neighbour, give yourself a bad time... and have to find it again in the end?

9 What you have just said, say it in another tone, without anger, and your argument will gain in strength, and, above all, you won't offend God.

10 Do not reprimand while you feel indignant about a fault committed. –Wait until the next day, or even longer. –And then, calmly and having purified your intention, do not neglect to make your reprimand. –You will gain more with one friendly word than with a three-hour quarrel. –Curb your temper.

11 Will-power. –Energy. –Example. –What has to be done, is done... Without wavering... Without giving in to human respect.

Otherwise, Cisneros* would not have been Cisneros; nor Teresa of Avila, Saint Teresa..., nor Iñigo of Loyola, Saint Ignatius...

God and daring! –*Regnare Christum volumus!* –We want Christ to reign!

12 Grow stronger in the face of obstacles. –God's grace will not fail you: *Inter*

---

* Cardinal Cisneros (1436-1517): Spanish, regent of the throne of Spain, and confessor to Queen Isabella the Catholic. He started the reform of the Church in Spain, anticipating what, years later, the Council of Trent would start for all Christendom. His courage and strength of character were widely known – Trans.

medium montium pertransibunt aquae! –You will pass through the mountains!

What does it matter that for the time being you have to curtail your activity if afterwards, like a spring which has been compressed, you will reach incomparably farther than you ever dreamed?

13 Get rid of those useless thoughts which, at the very least, make you waste your time.

14 Don't waste your energy and your time, which belong to God, throwing stones at dogs that might bark at you on your way. Disregard them.

15 Don't leave your work for tomorrow.

16 Falling in with the crowd? You!... one of the herd? You were born to be a leader! Among us there is no room for the lukewarm. Humble yourself and Christ will set you aflame again with fires of Love.

17 Don't succumb to that disease of character whose symptoms are inconstancy in everything, superficiality in action and

speech, scatterbrained ideas...: in a word, frivolity.

And the frivolity – don't forget this – which leads you to have those daily plans that are so empty ("so full of emptiness"), if you don't react in time – not tomorrow: now! – will make your life that of a dead and useless puppet.

18 You persist in being worldly, frivolous and scatterbrained because you are a coward. What is it but cowardice not to want to face up to yourself?

19 Will-power. It is a very important characteristic. Don't despise little things, for by the continual practice of saying no and denying yourself in such things – which are never futile, or trivial – you will, with God's grace, add strength and virility to your will, and so become very much master of yourself, first. And, then, a guide, a chief, a leader!..., to compel, and push, and draw others, with your example and with your word and with your knowledge and with your authority.

20 You have clashes of character with other people... That kind of thing is inevitable: you're not a gold coin that everyone likes.

Besides, without those clashes produced by your contact with your neighbour, how would you lose the rough edges and jagged points – the imperfections and defects – of your temper, so as to acquire the regular, polished and firmly gentle form of charity, of perfection?

If your character and the characters of those who live with you were soft and sweet like meringues, you would not become a saint.

21 Pretexts. –You'll never lack them if you want to avoid fulfilling your obligations. What a profusion of well-argued nonsense!

Don't stop to consider such nonsense. –Dismiss it and do your duty.

22 Be firm. –Be virile. –Be a man. –And then... be an angel.

23 What was that?... You can't do more!? –Couldn't it be that... you can't do less?

24 You are ambitious:... for knowledge..., for leadership..., for daring ventures.

Good. That's fine. –But... let it be for Christ, for Love.

25 Don't get into arguments. –Arguments usually don't produce light, because it gets extinguished by passion.

26 Marriage is a holy sacrament. –When the time comes, and you are making ready to receive it, ask your director or your confessor to suggest a suitable book. –And you will be better prepared to bear worthily the burdens of the home.

27 You laugh because I tell you that you have a "vocation to marriage"? –Well, you have: just that, a vocation.

Commend yourself to Saint Raphael, so that he may lead you chastely to the end of the journey, as he did Tobias.

28 Marriage is for the rank and file and not for the general staff of Christ. –For, whereas eating is necessary for each individual, begetting is necessary only for the

species, individual people can overlook it.

Longing for children?... Children, many children, and an indelible trail of light we shall leave behind us if we sacrifice the egoism of the flesh.

29 The relative and feeble happiness of the egoist, who withdraws into his ivory tower, into his shell..., is not difficult to attain in this world. –But the happiness of the egoist is not lasting.

Are you going to give up, for this caricature of heaven, the Happiness of Glory, which will have no end?

30 You are too calculating. –Don't tell me you are young. Youth gives all it can: it gives its very self without reserve.

31 You egoist. –You, always doing "your own thing". –You seem incapable of feeling the fraternity of Christ: in those around you, you do not see brothers; you see stepping stones.

I can foresee your complete downfall. –And when you are sunk low, you will want others to treat you with the charity that you are not willing to show them now.

32 You will not be a leader if, in the crowd, you see a mere footstool to help you climb higher. –You will be a leader if you are ambitious to save all mankind.

You can't turn your back on the crowds: you have to be eager to make them happy.

33 You never want to get to the bottom of the truth. –Sometimes, through politeness. Other times – most times – through not wanting to make life difficult for yourself. Sometimes again, through not wanting to make it so for others. And, always, through cowardice.

That way, with your fear of getting to the bottom of things, you will never be a man of sound judgement.

34 Don't be afraid of the truth, even though the truth may mean your death.

35 I don't like all this euphemism: your calling cowardice prudence. –For this "prudence" of yours gives the enemies of

God, with minds empty of ideas, the chance to pass themselves off as scholars and reach positions they should never have attained.

36 That abuse is not beyond remedy. –It shows lack of character to allow it to continue, as something hopeless and impossible to put right.

Don't shirk your duty. –Carry it out directly, even if others neglect theirs.

37 You're what they'd call a "smooth talker". –But, in spite of all your talk, you won't get me to justify – providential!, you called it – what has no justification.

38 Can it be true – no, no, I can't believe it – that in the world there are not men but bellies?

39 "Pray that I may never be satisfied with what is easy." –I have prayed. Now what's needed is for you to commit yourself to carry out that fine resolution.

40 Faith, cheerfulness, optimism. –But not the silliness of closing one's eyes to reality.

41 What a "profound" way of living a life of empty follies, of getting to be something in life – rising higher and higher – simply by "weighing little", by having nothing either in one's head or in one's heart!

42 Why that fitful character? When are you going to fix your will on something definite? –Give up your liking for foundation-stones and put the finishing touch to just one of your projects.

43 Don't be so... touchy. –You're hurt by the slightest thing. –One has to weigh one's words before speaking to you even about quite insignificant matters.

Don't be annoyed if I tell you that you are... unbearable. –Unless you correct your behaviour, you will never be useful.

44 Give the polite excuse which Christian charity and social convention demand. –And then, on your way again!, with holy shamelessness, without stopping until you have finally scaled the heights of duty.

45 Why are you hurt by the mistaken

assumptions people make about you? –You would be even worse, if God were to leave you. –Persevere in doing good, and shrug your shoulders.

46 Don't you think that equality, as some people understand it, is synonymous with injustice?

47 That pompous and self-satisfied manner doesn't suit you at all: it is obviously put on. –Try, at least, not to use it either with God, nor with your director, nor with your brothers: and there will be, between them and you, one barrier less.

48 You lack strength of character: how keen you are to get involved in everything! –You are bent on being the salt of every dish... And – you won't be annoyed if I tell you clearly – you have little aptitude to be salt: and you aren't able to dissolve and pass unnoticed, the way salt does.

You have too little spirit of sacrifice; and too great a spirit of curiosity and ostentation.

49 Check your tongue. –Don't be "baby-ish", a caricature of a child, telling tales, a mischief-maker, a little sneak. –With your stories and gossip you have chilled the glow of charity: you couldn't have done more harm, and... if by any chance you have shaken, with that wagging tongue of yours, the strong walls of other people's perseverance, your own perseverance is no longer a grace from God, for it has become a treacherous instrument of the enemy.

50 You are curious and inquisitive, prying and nosey: aren't you ashamed that even in your defects you're so unmanly? –Be a man: and those desires you have to know about other people's lives, replace them by desires and a real effort to get to know yourself.

51 Your manly spirit, simple and straightforward, feels oppressed when it finds itself entangled in gossip and mischievous talk, which it cannot really explain and in which it never wished to get involved. –Undergo the humiliation which such talk causes you, and let the ordeal teach you greater discretion.

52 Why, when judging others, do you put into your criticism the bitterness of your own failures?

53 That critical spirit – I grant that it is not gossip – you shouldn't exercise it upon your apostolate, nor upon your brothers. –That critical spirit, as far as your supernatural undertaking is concerned – you don't mind if I tell you this? – is a great hindrance, for when you go about examining the work of the others, without there being any reason why you should do so – with the highest possible motives, I grant – you are not doing anything constructive but rather, with your passive approach, you are putting a brake on the progress of all.

"But then," you ask, uneasily, "that critical spirit which is like the keynote of my character...?"

Listen. I'll set your mind at rest. Take a pen and a sheet of paper. Write down simply and trustingly – ah! and briefly – the things that are worrying you, hand the note to your superior, and don't think any more about it. –He, as the person in charge, he has the grace of state, and he will file the note... or throw it into the waste-paper basket. –To you, since your critical spirit is not gossip and you're acting from the highest motives, it is all the same.

54 Compromise? –It's a word found only ("One must compromise!") in the vocabulary of those who have no will to fight – the easy-lifers, the sly or the cowardly – because they know they are beaten even before they begin.

55 My dear man: be a little less ingenuous (even though you feel very much a child, and even though you are one before God) and don't put your brothers "on the spot" in front of strangers.

DIRECTION

56 "The stuff of saints." –You hear this said of some people: that they have the stuff of saints. –Apart from the fact that the saints were not made of "stuff", having the raw material is not enough.

One needs to be very obedient to the Director and very docile to grace. –Because, if we don't allow God's grace and the Director to do their work, there will never appear the finished sculpture, the image of Jesus, into which the saintly man is fashioned.

And the "stuff of saints" we were speaking of will be no more than a rough, unshaped log, fit for the fire... for a good fire if it was good stuff!

57 Get to know the Holy Spirit – the Great Unknown – for it is he who is to sanctify you.

Don't forget that you are God's temple. –The Paraclete is in the centre of your soul: listen to him and be docile to his inspirations.

58 Don't hinder the work of the Paraclete: unite yourself to Christ, so as to be purified, and feel, with Him, the insults, and the spitting, and the blows..., and the thorns, and the weight of the cross..., and the iron nails tearing your flesh, and the anguish of a forsaken death...

And enter into Our Lord Jesus' open side until you find sure refuge in his wounded Heart.

59 It's good for you to know this sound teaching: one's own mind is a bad adviser, a poor pilot, to steer the soul in the storms and tempests, among the reefs of the interior life.

That is why it is God's Will that the command of the ship be entrusted to a Master so that, with his light and knowledge, he can guide us to a safe harbour.

60 If you wouldn't build, without an architect, a good house to live in, here on earth, how then can you hope, without a Director, to build the castle of your sanctification to live eternally in heaven?

61 When a layman sets himself up as an expert on morals he often makes mistakes: laymen can only be disciples.

62 A Director. –You need one. –In order to surrender yourself, to give yourself..., by obedience. –And a Director who understands your apostolate, who knows what God wants: that way he will further the work of the Holy Spirit in your soul effectively, without taking you out of your place..., filling you with peace, and showing you how to make your work fruitful.

63 You – you think – you have a lot of personality: your studies – your research work, your publications –, your social standing – your family background –, your political activities – the positions you hold –,

your wealth..., your age, you're no longer a child!...

Precisely because of all that, you, more than others, need a Director for your soul.

64 Don't hide from your Director those insinuations of the enemy. –Your victory, in taking him into your confidence, brings you more grace from God. –And moreover you now have, to help you keep on conquering, the gift of counsel and the prayers of your spiritual father.

65 Why that reluctance to see yourself and to let yourself be seen by your Director as you really are?

You will have won a great battle if you lose that fear of letting yourself be known.

66 The Priest – whoever he may be – is always another Christ.

67 Though you may well know it, I want to remind you again that the Priest is "another Christ". –And that the Holy Spirit has said: *Nolite tangere Christos meos,* Do not venture to touch "my Christs".

68 Presbyter, etymologically, denotes an old man. –If old age deserves veneration, think how much more you ought to venerate the Priest.

69 It shows very little spiritual refinement – and a great lack of respect – to poke fun at or make remarks about the Priest – whoever he may be – no matter what the pretext!

70 I insist: to make fun of – to mock – the Priest, no matter what the circumstances which make it excusable in your eyes, is always, at the very least, a sign of coarseness and vulgarity.

71 How much we should admire priestly purity! –It is their treasure. –No tyrant will ever be able to wrest this crown from the Church.

72 Don't place the Priest in peril of losing his dignity. It is a virtue which, without being pompous, he simply must have.

How earnestly it was prayed for – "Lord, grant me... eighty years of gravity!" – by that young cleric and friend of ours!

You too pray for it, for the Priesthood everywhere, and you will have done a good thing.

73 It hurt you – like a dagger in your heart – to hear people say that you had spoken badly of those priests. –And I am glad that you were hurt: now I am quite sure you have the right spirit!

74 To love God and not revere the Priest... is not possible.

75 Like the good sons of Noah, cover with the cloak of charity the defects you may see in your father, the Priest.

76 If you don't have a plan of life, you'll never have order.

77 This tying oneself to a plan of life, to a timetable, you told me, is so monotonous! And I answered you: There is monotony because there is little Love.

78 If you don't get up at a fixed time you will never carry out your plan of life.

79 Virtue without order? –Strange virtue!

80 When you bring order into your life your time will multiply and, as a result, you will be able to give greater glory to God, by working more in his service.

PRAYER

81 Action is worth nothing without prayer: prayer grows in value with sacrifice.

82 First, prayer; then, expiation; in the third place, very much in the “third place”, action.

83 Prayer is the foundation of the spiritual edifice. –Prayer is all-powerful.

84 *Domine, doce nos orare* –Lord, teach us how to pray! –And Our Lord replied: When you pray, you are to say: *Pater noster, qui es in coelis...* –Our Father, who art in heaven...

How can we fail to appreciate the value of vocal prayer!

85 Slowly. –Consider what you are saying, who is saying it and to whom. –For that hurried talk, without time for reflection, is just noise, the clatter of tin cans.

And, with Saint Teresa, I will tell you that, however much you work your lips, I do not call it prayer.

86 Your prayer should be liturgical. –I would like to see you growing fond of reciting the psalms, and prayers from the missal, rather than private or special prayers.

87 "Man does not live on bread alone, but on every word that proceeds from the mouth of God," said Our Lord. –Bread and word!: Host and prayer.

Otherwise, you won't live a supernatural life.

88 You seek the company of friends who, with their conversation and affection, with their friendship, make the exile of this world more bearable for you..., although friends sometimes let one down. –I don't think it's wrong to do that.

But... how is it that you don't frequent daily with greater intensity the company, the conversation with the Great Friend, who never lets one down?

89 "Mary chose the better part", we read in the Holy Gospel. –There she is, drinking in the words of the Master. Apparently inactive, she is praying and loving. –Afterwards she accompanies Jesus in his preaching through towns and villages.

Without prayer, how difficult it is to accompany him!

90 You say you don't know how to pray? –Place yourself in the presence of God, and as soon as you begin to say: "Lord, I don't know how to pray!...", rest assured that you have begun to do so.

91 You wrote to me: "To pray is to talk with God. But about what?" –About what? About Him, about yourself: joys, sorrows, successes and failures, noble ambitions, daily worries... weaknesses!: and acts of thanksgiving and petitions: and Love and reparation.

In short: to get to know him and to

get to know yourself – "to get acquainted!"

92 *Et in meditatione mea exardescit ignis* –And, in my meditation, a fire flames up. –That is why you go to pray: to become a bonfire, a living flame, giving heat and light.

So, when you are not able to go on, when you feel that your fire is dying out, if you cannot throw on it sweet-smelling logs, throw on the branches and twigs of little vocal prayers, of ejaculations, to keep the bonfire burning. –And you will have used your time well.

93 You see yourself so wretched that you acknowledge you are unworthy to be heard by God... But, what about the merits of Mary? And the wounds of your Lord? And moreover... are you not a son of God?

Besides, He listens to you *quoniam bonus..., quoniam in saeculum misericordia eius* – because he is good, because his mercy endures for ever.

94 He has become so small –you see: a Child!– so that you can approach him with confidence.

95 *In te, Domine, speravi*: In thee, Lord, have I hoped. –And I put in, together with human resources, my prayer and my cross. –And my hope was not in vain, nor will it ever be: *Non confundar in aeternum!* – I shall never be disappointed!

96 Jesus speaks: “Amen I say to you: ask, and you shall receive; seek, and you shall find; knock and it shall be opened to you.”

Pray. In what human venture can you have greater guarantees of success?

97 You don’t know what to say to Our Lord in your prayer. You can’t remember anything, and yet you would like to consult him on many things. –Look: make some notes during the day of the points you would like to consider in the presence of God. And then take those notes with you to pray.

98 After the prayer of the Priest and of consecrated virgins, the prayer most pleasing to God is that of children and that of the sick.

99 When you go to pray, let this be a firm

resolution: neither more time because it's been consoling, nor less because it's been dry.

100 Don't tell Jesus that you want consolation in prayer. –If he gives it to you, thank him for it. –Tell him always that you want perseverance.

101 Persevere in prayer. –Persevere, even if your efforts seem barren. –Prayer is always fruitful.

102 Your mind is sluggish and won't work: you struggle in vain to collect your thoughts in God's presence: there's a complete blank!

Don't try to force yourself, and don't worry. –Listen to me: the time has come for your heart to take over.

103 Those words, which struck you when you were at prayer, engrave them in your memory and recite them slowly many times during the day.

104 *Pernoctans in oratione Dei* – he

spent the night in prayer. –So Saint Luke says to us, of Our Lord.

And you? How many times have you persevered like that? –Well, then...

105 If you don't keep in touch with Christ in prayer and in the Bread, how will you make him known to others?

106 You've written to me, and I understand you well: "Every day I do my 'little bit' of prayer: if it weren't for that!"

107 A saint, without prayer?... –I don't believe in such sanctity.

108 I will tell you, borrowing a phrase from a foreign author, that your apostolic life is worth what your prayer is worth.

109 If you're not a man of prayer, I don't believe in the sincerity of your intentions when you say that you work for Christ.

110 You have told me sometimes that you are like a badly adjusted clock, which strikes at the wrong time: you are cold, dry and arid at the time of your prayer; and, on the other hand, when it is least to be expected, in the street, in your daily activities, in the midst of the bustle and hubbub of the city, or in the concentrated calm of your professional work, you find yourself praying... At the wrong time? Possibly; but don't let those chimes of your clock go to waste. –The spirit breathes where it will.

111 You made me laugh with your... impatient prayer. –You were saying to him: "I don't want to grow old, Jesus... To have to wait so long to see you! Then, perhaps I won't have a heart as inflamed as mine is now. To wait till I'm old seems too late. Now, my union would be more ardent, because I love you with the pure Love of youth."

112 I like to see you living that "ambitious reparation": "For the world!" you told me. –Fine. But, first of all, for the members of your supernatural family and your relatives, for the people of the country that is our Fatherland.

113 You were saying to him: "You mustn't trust me... Me, I certainly trust you, Jesus... I abandon myself in your arms: there I leave all I have, my wretchedness!" –And I think it is a good prayer.

114 The prayer of a Christian is never a monologue.

115 "Minutes of silence." –Leave them for those whose hearts are dry.

We Catholics, children of God, speak with our Father who is in heaven.

116 Don't neglect your spiritual reading. –Reading has made many saints.

117 In my spiritual reading – you write to me – I build up a store of fuel. –It looks like a lifeless heap, but often it is from there that my memory spontaneously draws material, which fills my prayer with life and inflames my thanksgiving after Communion.

HOLY PURITY

118 Holy purity is given by God when it is asked for with humility.

119 How beautiful is holy purity! But it is not holy, nor pleasing to God, if we separate it from charity.

Charity is the seed that will grow and yield delicious fruit under the fertile rain of purity.

Without charity, purity is barren, and its sterile waters turn souls into a quagmire, a pool of filth, from which rises the stench of pride.

120 "Purity?" they ask. And they smile. –They are the very people who approach marriage with withered bodies and disillusioned hearts.

I promise you a book – if God helps me – which could perhaps have this title: "Celibacy, Marriage and Purity".

121 There is need for a crusade of manliness and purity to counteract and undo the savage work of those who think that man is a beast.

–And that crusade is a matter for you.

122 Many live like angels in the midst of the world. –You... why not you?

123 When you make up your mind firmly to lead a clean life, chastity will not be a burden for you: it will be a triumphal crown.

124 You, a doctor and apostle, wrote to me: "We all know from experience that we can be chaste, living vigilantly, frequenting the Sacraments and stamping out the first sparks of passion before the fire gets a hold. And it is precisely among the chaste that are found the finest men, from every point of view. And among the lustful abound the timid, the selfish, the cheats and the cruel, which are characteristic features of little manliness."

125 How I wish – you told me – that John, the adolescent apostle, would take me into his confidence and give me advice: and encourage me to acquire purity of heart.

If you really want it, tell him so: and you'll feel encouraged and you'll get advice.

126 Gluttony is the forerunner of impurity.

127 Don't try to dialogue with concupiscence: despise it.

128 Bashfulness and modesty are younger brothers of purity.

129 Without holy purity one cannot persevere in the apostolate.

130 Rid me, Jesus, of that filthy crust of sensual corruption which covers my heart, so that I can feel and readily follow the touches of the Paraclete on my soul.

131 Never speak, not even to lament them, of impure things or events. –Remember that such matter is stickier than tar. –Change the subject or, if that's not possible, continue with it, speaking of the need and beauty of holy purity, a virtue of men who know what their souls are worth.

132 Don't be such a coward as to be "brave": flee!

133 The saints were not deformed beings; cases to be studied by some modernist doctor.

They were, they are, normal: of flesh, like yours. –And they conquered.

134 "Flesh... though dressed in silk." –That's what I'll tell you, when I see you waver before the temptation that hides its impurity under pretexts of art, of science..., of charity!

I'll tell you, with the words of an old Spanish proverb: "Flesh is flesh though dressed in silk."

135 If only you knew what you are

worth!... –It is Saint Paul who tells you: you have been purchased *pretio magno* – at a great price.

And then he says to you: *Glorificate et portate Deum in corpore vestro* – Glorify God and bear him in your body.

136 When you have sought the company of a sensual satisfaction... what loneliness afterwards!

137 And to think that for just a moment's satisfaction, which left in you bitter dregs of gall and aloes, you have lost "the way"!

138 *Infelix ego homo! Quis me liberabit de corpore mortis huius?* "Unhappy man that I am! Who will deliver me from this body of death?" –Thus cried Saint Paul. –Take courage: he too had to fight.

139 At the time of temptation think of the Love that awaits you in heaven: foster the virtue of hope, which is not a lack of generosity.

140 Don't worry, no matter what happens,

as long as you don't consent. –For only the will can open the door of the heart and let those vile things in.

141 You seem to hear a voice within you actually saying: "That religious prejudice!"... –And then the eloquent defence of all the wretchedness of our poor fallen flesh: "Its rights!"

If this happens to you tell the enemy that there is natural law and God's law, and... God! –And also hell.

142 *Domine!* – "Lord!" – *si vis, potes me mundare* – "If thou wilt, thou canst make me clean."

–What a beautiful prayer to say often, with the faith of the poor leper, should there happen to you what God and you and I know! –You won't have to wait long to hear the Master's reply: *Volo, mundare!* –"I will: be thou made clean!"

143 To defend his purity, Saint Francis of Assisi rolled in the snow, Saint Benedict threw himself into a thorn bush, Saint Bernard plunged into an icy pond... –You...

what have you done?

144 The spotless purity of John's whole life makes him strong at the Cross. –The rest of the apostles flee from Golgotha: he, with the Mother of Christ, remains.

–Don't forget that purity strengthens and invigorates character.

145 The Madrid battle-front. A score of officers, in noble and cheerful comradeship. A song is heard, then another, and another...

That young lieutenant with the brown moustache only heard the first:

"Divided hearts
are of no use to me.
If I give mine,
I'll give it whole to thee."

"What reluctance to give my heart entirely!" –And his prayer welled up in a broad and peaceful flow.

HEART

146 You give me the impression that you are carrying your heart in your hands, as if you were offering goods for sale: Who wants it? –If it takes no creature's fancy, you will come and give it to God.

Do you think that is how the saints acted?

147 Creatures for you? –Creatures are for God: at most, for you through God.

148 Why stoop to drink in the puddles of worldly consolations when you can quench your thirst in waters that spring up into life everlasting?

149 Detach yourself from creatures until

you are stripped of them. For, says Pope Saint Gregory, the devil has nothing of his own in this world, and naked he comes into battle. If you go clothed to fight him, you will soon fall to the ground: for he will have something to catch you by.

150 It's as if your Angel were saying to you: "You have your heart so full of human attachments!..." –And then: "Is that, what you want your Guardian to guard?"

151 Detachment. –How hard it is!... Oh to be fastened by nothing but three nails and to feel nothing in my flesh but the Cross!

152 Don't you have a feeling that greater peace and closer union will come to you when you have responded to that extraordinary grace which is asking you for total detachment?

–Struggle for His sake, to please Him: but strengthen your hope.

153 Go on, ask him generously and like a child: "What can you mean to give me when you are asking 'this' thing of me?"

154 You're afraid of becoming cold and distant towards everyone. You want so very much to be detached!

–Forget that worry: if you belong to Christ – entirely to Christ! – you will have for everyone – from Christ himself – fire, light and warmth.

155 Jesus isn't satisfied "going halves": he wants everything.

156 You don't want to tie yourself to God's Will... yet you go along, instead, with the will of any pathetic little creature.

157 Don't get things out of joint: if God himself gives himself to you, how can you be so attached to creatures?

158 Now it's tears. –It hurts, does it? –Of course, it does!: that's precisely why you have been hit there.

159 Your heart weakens and you clutch at some earthly support. –Fine; but take care that what you grasp to stop you from falling doesn't become a dead weight dragging you down, a chain enslaving you.

160 Tell me, honestly: is that... a friendship, or is it a chain?

161 You pour out your tenderness lavishly. –And I say to you: charity towards your neighbours, yes: always. –But – listen carefully to me, apostolic soul – for Christ, and for Him alone, is that other feeling which Our Lord himself has placed in your heart. –Besides... isn't it true that drawing back any one of the bolts of your heart – and you need seven bolts – has more than once left a little cloud of doubt floating on your supernatural horizon..., and then, tormented in spite of the purity of your intentions, you have wondered: Haven't I gone too far in my outward expressions of affection?

162 Leave your heart aside. First comes duty. –But, in fulfilling your duty, put your heart into that fulfilment: it smooths the way.

163 If your right eye scandalises you... pluck it out and cast it from you! –Your poor heart... that's what scandalises you!

Press it, squeeze it tight in your hands: don't give it consolations. –And, filled with a noble compassion, when it asks for them, say to it slowly, as one speaking in confidence: "Heart: heart on the Cross! Heart on the Cross!"

164 How is that heart of yours getting along? –Let me not see you worry: the saints – who were normal, well-adjusted people, like you and me – also felt those "natural" inclinations. And if they had not felt them, their "supernatural" reaction of keeping their heart – soul and body – for God, instead of giving it to one of his creatures, would have had little merit.

Therefore, once the way has been seen, I think that the heart's weakness shouldn't be an obstacle for a soul that is determined and "fully in love".

165 You... who for a feeble little earthly love have put up with so many low and mean experiences, can you really believe that you love Christ when you're not willing – for His sake! – to go through this humiliation?

166 You write to me: "Father, I've got... toothache in my heart." –I won't laugh, because I can see that you need a good dentist to do a few extractions for you.

If only you were willing!...

167 "If only I had broken it off at the start!" you told me. –Let us hope you won't have to repeat that belated exclamation.

168 "I was amused to hear you speak of the 'account' that Our Lord will demand of you. No, for none of you will he be a Judge, in the harsh sense of the word; he will be simply Jesus." –This phrase, written by a holy Bishop, which has consoled more than one troubled heart, could very well console yours.

169 Suffering overwhelms you because you receive it like a coward. –Receive it bravely, with a Christian spirit: and you will come to esteem it as a treasure.

170 How clear the way is!... How obvious the obstacles!... What good weapons to overcome them!... –And yet, how much going astray and how much stumbling! That's so, isn't it?

–It's that fine thread – a chain: a chain of wrought iron – which you and I know about, and which you aren't willing to break, and it is causing you to stray from the path, and making you stumble and even fall.

–What are you waiting for to cut it... and go forward?

171 His Love... is well worth any love!

MORTIFICATION

172 If you are not mortified you will never be a soul of prayer.

173 That witty remark, the joke held on the tip of your tongue; the cheerful smile for someone who annoys you; that silence when you're unjustly accused; your friendly conversation with people you find boring and tactless; the daily effort to overlook one irritating or impertinent detail after another in the persons who live with you... This, with perseverance, is indeed solid interior mortification.

174 Don't say: "That person gets on my nerves." –Think: "That person is making a saint of me."

175 No ideal becomes a reality without sacrifice. –Deny yourself. –It's so beautiful to be a victim!

176 How many times you resolve to serve God in something... and you have to content yourself, you're such a miserable wretch, with offering him the peeved feeling of having failed to keep such a simple resolution!

177 Don't miss the opportunity of sacrificing your own judgement. –It's hard... but, how pleasing it is in the eyes of God!

178 When you see a poor wooden Cross, alone, uncared for and of no value... and without its Crucified, don't forget that that Cross is your Cross: the Cross of each day, the hidden Cross, without splendour or consolation..., which is awaiting the Crucified it lacks: and that Crucified must be you.

179 Look for mortifications that don't mortify others.

180 Where there is no mortification there

is no virtue.

181 Interior mortification. –I don't believe in your interior mortification if I see that you disregard, that you don't practise, mortification of the senses.

182 Let us drink to the last drop the chalice of pain in this poor present life. –What does it matter to suffer for ten years, twenty, fifty... if afterwards there is heaven for ever, for ever... for ever?

–And, above all – rather than for the reason I've given, *propter retributionem,* because of the reward – what does suffering matter if we suffer to console, to please God Our Lord, in a spirit of reparation, united to Him on his Cross – in a word, if we suffer for Love?...

183 The eyes! Through them many iniquities enter the soul. –How many experiences like David's!... –If you guard your sight you will have assured the custody of your heart.

184 Why look around, when you're

carrying "your world" within you?

185 The world admires only spectacular sacrifice, because it does not know the value of sacrifice that is hidden and silent.

186 We must give ourselves entirely, we must deny ourselves entirely: our sacrifice must be a holocaust.

187 Paradox: To Live one must die.

188 Remember that the heart is a traitor. –Keep it locked with seven bolts.

189 Everything that does not lead you to God is a hindrance. Tear it out and throw it far away.

190 A soul whose immediate superior was a rough and irritable type was moved by God to say: "Thank you, my God, for this truly divine treasure, for where would I find another who for every kindness I do answers me back with a couple of kicks?"

191 Conquer yourself each day from the

very first moment, getting up on the dot, at a fixed time, without conceding a single minute to laziness.

If, with God's help, you conquer yourself, you will be well ahead for the rest of the day.

It's so demoralising to feel oneself beaten in the first skirmish!

192 You always come out beaten. –Propose to yourself, each time, the salvation of a particular soul, or his sanctification, or his vocation to the apostolate... –That way I am certain of your victory.

193 I don't want you weak and soft. –It's about time you got rid of that strange compassion you feel for yourself.

194 I am going to tell you which are man's treasures on earth so that you won't let them go to waste: hunger, thirst, heat, cold, pain, dishonour, poverty, loneliness, betrayal, slander, prison...

195 It has been fittingly said that the soul and the body are two enemies who can't get away from one another, and two friends who can't bear the sight of each other.

196 The body should be given a little less than its due. If not, it turns traitor.

197 If they have witnessed your weaknesses and failures, what does it matter if they witness your penance?

198 These are the delicious fruits of the mortified soul: understanding and tolerance for the defects of others; intolerance for one's own.

199 If the grain of wheat does not die, it remains unfruitful. –Don't you want to be a grain of wheat, to die through mortification, and to yield stalks ripe with grain? –May Jesus bless your wheat field!

200 You don't conquer yourself, you aren't mortified, because you are proud. –You lead a life of penance? Don't forget that pride is compatible with penance... –Furthermore: your sorrow, after you've fallen, after your failures in generosity, is it true sorrow or petty annoyance at seeing yourself so small and weak? –How far you are from Jesus, if you are not humble... even though your disciplines may be producing fresh roses daily!

201 What a taste of gall and vinegar, of ash and aloes! What a parched, coated and cracked palate! –And this physical feeling seems as nothing compared with that other bad taste in your soul.

–The fact is that "more is being asked of you" and you can't bring yourself to give it. –Humble yourself: would that bitter unpleasant impression remain, in your flesh and in your spirit, if you were doing all you could?

202 So you're going to impose some voluntary punishment on yourself for your weakness and lack of generosity? –Very well: but let it be a discreet penance, imposed, as it were, on an enemy who is at the same time our brother.

203 The joy of us poor humans, even when it has a supernatural motive, always leaves an aftertaste of bitterness. –What did you expect? –Here below, suffering is the salt of our life.

204 How many, who would let themselves be nailed to a cross before the astonished gaze of thousands of spectators, cannot bear with a Christian spirit the pinpricks of each day! –Think, then, which is the more heroic.

205 We were reading – you and I – the heroically ordinary life of that man of God. –And we saw him struggle, for months and years (what "accounts" he kept in his particular examination!), at breakfast time: today he won, tomorrow he was beaten... He noted down: "Didn't take butter..., did take butter!"

May we too – you and I – live our... "butter tragedy".

206 The heroic minute. –It's the time fixed for getting up: on the dot. Without hesitation: a supernatural thought and... up! –The heroic minute: here you have a mortification that strengthens your will and doesn't weaken your body.

207 Give thanks, as for a very special favour, for that holy abhorrence you feel for yourself.

PENANCE

208 Let us bless pain. –Love pain. –Sanctify pain... Glorify pain!

209 A whole programme, for us to study with profit the "subject" of suffering, is given to us by the Apostle: *spe gaudentes* – be happy through hope, *in tribulatione patientes* – be patient in tribulation, *orationi instantes* – be constant in prayer.

210 Expiation: this is the path that leads to Life.

211 Bury with your penance, in the deep pit which your humility will have opened up, your negligences, offences and sins. –Just so the gardener buries, at the foot of the very tree that bore them, rotten fruit, dried twigs and dead leaves. –And what was useless, or rather, what was harmful, makes a real contribution to a new fruitfulness.

Learn to draw, from falls, an impulse: from death, life.

212 That Christ, whom you're seeing, is not Jesus. –At best it may be a pitiful image that your blurred eyes manage to form... –Purify yourself. Clarify your sight with humility and penance. Then... the clean lights of Love will not be denied you. And you will have perfect vision. The image you see will be really his: Him!

213 Jesus suffers to fulfil the Will of the Father... And you, who also wish to fulfil the most Holy Will of God, following in the footsteps of the Master, can you complain if you meet suffering as a travelling companion?

214 Tell your body: I prefer to keep you in slavery than be myself your slave.

215 How afraid people are of atonement!

If the things they do to keep up appearances, were done with a purified intention, for God's sake... what saints some men and women would be!

216 You are crying? –Don't be ashamed of it. Yes, cry: for men also cry, like you, when they are alone and before God. –At night, says King David, I will bathe my couch with tears.

With those burning and manly tears, you can purify your past and supernaturalise your present life.

217 I want you to be happy on earth. –But you won't be if you don't lose that fear of suffering. For, as long as we are "wayfarers", it is precisely in suffering that our happiness lies.

218 How beautiful it is to lose this life for the sake of Life!

219 If you realise that those sufferings – physical or moral – mean purification and merit, bless them.

220 Aren't you left with a bad taste in your mouth by that wish for physiological well-being – "God give you health, brother" – with which some beggars show gratitude or call out for alms?

221 If we are generous in our voluntary expiation, Jesus will fill us with grace to love the expiations He may send us.

222 Let your will exact from your senses, by means of expiation, what your other faculties deny it in prayer.

223 How little penance is worth without constant mortification!

224 You are afraid of penance?... Of penance, which will help you obtain everlasting Life. –And yet you see how, in order to preserve this poor present life, people will submit to the thousand tortures of a gory surgical operation?

225 Your worst enemy is yourself.

226 Treat your body with charity, but

with no more charity than one would show towards a treacherous enemy.

227 If you know that your body is your enemy, and an enemy of God's glory, since it is an enemy of your sanctification, why do you treat it so softly?

228 "Have a good evening," they said to us, as people usually do. And the comment of a soul very close to God was: "What limited wishes some people have!"

229 With you, Jesus, how pleasurable is suffering and how luminous is darkness!

230 You are suffering! –Well, look: "His" Heart isn't smaller than ours. –You are suffering? Then it must be good for you.

231 Strict fasting is a penance most pleasing to God. –But, what with one thing and another, we have become a bit too easy-going. There is no objection – quite the contrary – if you, with your Director's approval, practise it frequently.

232 Motives for penance?: Atonement, reparation, petition, thanksgiving: a means to go forward...: for you, for me, for the others, for your family, for your country, for the Church... And a thousand motives more.

233 Don't do more penance than your Director allows you.

234 How we ennoble suffering, when we put it in its proper place (expiation) in the economy of the spirit!

EXAMINATION OF CONSCIENCE

235 Examination of conscience. –A daily task. –Book-keeping is never neglected by anyone in business.

And is there any business more important than the business of eternal life?

236 At the time of your examination beware of the dumb devil.

237 Examine yourself: slowly, courageously. –Isn't it true that your bad humour and your gloominess, both of them without cause – without apparent cause – are due to your lack of determination to break the subtle, but "specific" snares laid for you – cunningly, and soothingly – by your concupiscence?

238 The general examination of conscience is like defence. –The particular, like attack. –The first is one's armour. The second, a sword of Toledo steel.

239 A look back at the past. To... bewail it? No: that's useless. –To learn: which is fruitful.

240 Ask for light. –Insist: until you get to the root and can then get at it with your weapon of attack, the particular examination.

241 With your particular examination you ought to go straight towards acquiring a definite virtue or uprooting the defect which is dominating you.

242 "How much I'm indebted to God, for being a Christian: my lack of response, given such a debt, has made me weep with sorrow: with sorrow of Love. *Mea culpa!*" –It is good that you are beginning to acknowledge your debts: but don't forget how they are paid: with tears... and with deeds.

243 *Qui fidelis est in minimo et in majori fidelis est* –he who is faithful in what is

little is also faithful in what is great. –These are words of Saint Luke which show you – examine yourself – the root cause of your strayings.

244 React. –Listen to what the Holy Spirit is saying to you: *Si inimicus meus maledixisset mihi, sustinuissem utique* – if my enemy offends me, it is not surprising, and it's more easily tolerated. But you... *tu vero homo unanimis, dux meus, et notus meus, qui simul mecum dulces capiebas cibos* – you!, my friend, my apostle, who sit at my table and take sweet food with me!

245 On retreat days your examination should be deeper and more thorough than the usual few minutes at night. –Otherwise, you miss a great chance of putting things right.

246 Always end your examination with an act of Love – of sorrow of Love: for yourself, for all the sins of mankind... –And consider God's fatherly care of you, who removed the obstacles so that you would not stumble.

RESOLUTIONS

247 Be specific. –Don't let your resolutions be like fireworks that sparkle for an instant, only to leave behind as a bitter reality a blackened useless stub to be thrown away in disgust.

248 You are so young! –To me you are like a ship setting out on its voyage. –That slight deviation now, if you don't correct it, will mean that in the end you won't reach your destination.

249 Make few resolutions. –Make specific resolutions. –And fulfil them with the help of God.

250 You said to me, and I listened to you

in silence: "Yes: I want to be a saint." Even though an assertion such as this, so broad and vague, would as a rule seem nonsense to me.

251 "Tomorrow!": sometimes it may be prudence; very often it is the adverb of the defeated.

252 Make this firm and determined resolution: to recall, when you receive honours and praise, the things that make you blush and feel ashamed.

These things are yours; the praise and glory, God's.

253 Behave well "now", without remembering "yesterday", which has already passed, or worrying about "tomorrow", which for all you know may never come for you.

254 Now! Return to that noble life of yours now. –Don't let yourself be fooled: "now" is not too soon... nor too late.

255 Do you want me to tell you everything I think about "your way"? –Very well then, as I see it, if you respond to the call, you'll work for Christ like the best: if you become a man of prayer, you *will* respond as I've described and, hungry for sacrifice, you will seek the hardest tasks...

And you will be happy here, and most happy hereafter, in everlasting Life.

256 That wound hurts. –But it's on the mend: stick to your resolutions. And soon the pain will turn into joyous peace.

257 You are like a sand-bag. –You're not making any effort to contribute. So no wonder you are beginning to feel the symptoms of lukewarmness. –React!

SCRUPLES

258 Get rid of those scruples that take away your peace. –What robs a person's peace of soul does not come from God.

When God comes to you, you will sense the truth of those greetings: Peace I give to you..., peace I leave with you..., peace be with you..., and this, in the midst of tribulation.

259 Still with those scruples! –Speak simply and clearly to your Director.

Obey... and don't belittle Our Lord's most loving Heart.

260 Gloominess, depression. I am not surprised: it's the cloud of dust raised by your fall. But... that's enough! Can't you

see that the cloud has been borne far away by the breath of grace?

Moreover, your gloominess – if you don't reject it – could very well be the cloak of your pride. –Did you really think you were perfect and incapable of sinning?

261 I forbid you to think any more about it. –Instead, bless God, who has given back life to your soul.

262 Don't think any more about your fall. –That thought, as well as covering you and pressing upon you like a slab of stone, may easily give rise to further temptations. –Christ has forgiven you: forget the "old man".

263 Don't lose heart. –I have seen you struggle...: your defeat today is training for final victory.

264 You've done well..., even though you have fallen so low. –You've done well, because you humbled yourself, because you put things right, because you filled yourself with hope, and that hope brought you back again to his Love. –Don't look so amazed: you've really done well! –You got up from the ground: *Surge*, –Arise, the mighty voice once again cried, – *et ambula!*: and now, to work!

PRESENCE OF GOD

265 Children... How hard they try to behave properly when they're in front of their parents.

And the children of Kings, before their father the King, how hard they try to uphold the royal dignity!

And you... don't you know you are always before the Great King, your Father-God?

266 Never make a decision without stopping to consider the matter in the presence of God.

267 It's necessary to become convinced that God is close beside us all the time. –We live as though the Lord were far away, in the starlit heavens, and we don't consider that he is also always by our side.

And he is here like a loving Father – he loves each one of us more than all the mothers in the world can love their children – helping us, inspiring us, blessing... and forgiving.

How often we have cleared a frown from our parents' brows by telling them, after some misdemeanour: "I won't do it any more!" –Maybe that very day we fell once more... –And our father, with feigned harshness in his voice and a serious face, reprimands us..., while in his heart he is moved, realising our weakness, thinking: "Poor child, how hard he tries to behave well!"

We need to be imbued, to be saturated with the knowledge that the Lord, who is close beside us and in heaven, is our Father and very much our Father.

268 Get used to raising up your heart to God, in acts of thanksgiving, many times a day. –Because he gives you this thing and that. –Because you have been despised. –Because you haven't got what you need or because you do have it.

Because he made his Mother, who is also your Mother, so beautiful. –Because he created the Sun and the Moon and this animal and that plant. –Because he made that man eloquent and you he made slow of speech...

Give him thanks for everything, because everything is good.

269 Don't be so blind or so thoughtless as not to enter inside each Tabernacle when you glimpse the walls or towers of the houses of God. –He is waiting for you.

Don't be so blind or so thoughtless as not to pray to Mary Immaculate, with an ejaculation at least, when you pass near places where you know Christ is offended.

270 Doesn't it make you happy if you discover, along your usual route through the streets of the city, another Tabernacle!?

271 A soul of prayer was saying: in intentions, may Jesus be our end; in affections, our Love; in speech, our theme; in actions, our model.

272 Make use of those holy "human devices" that I suggested to help you not lose your presence of God: ejaculations, acts of Love and reparation, spiritual Communions, "glances" at a picture of Our Lady...

273 Alone! –You are not alone. We are keeping you close company from afar. –Besides..., abiding in your soul in grace is the Holy Spirit – God with you – who is giving a supernatural tone to all your thoughts, desires and actions.

274 "Father," said that big fellow, a good student at the Central University* (I wonder what has become of him), "I was thinking of what you told me... that I'm a son of God!, and I found myself walking along the street, head up, chin out, and a proud feeling inside... a son of God!"

With sure conscience I advised him to foster that "pride".

275 I don't doubt your good intentions. –I know that you act in the presence of

---

* This was the name of the University of Madrid at the time *The Way* was written. –Trans.

God. But (and there is a "but"!), your actions are witnessed or may be witnessed by men who judge by human standards... And you must give them good example.

276 If you accustom yourself, even if it's only once a week, to seek union with Mary in order to go to Jesus, you will see how you have more presence of God.

277 You ask me: why that wooden Cross? –And I copy from a letter: "As I look up from the microscope, my eyes fall upon the black and empty Cross. This Cross without its Crucified is a symbol. It has a meaning which others won't see. And I who was tired out, and on the point of stopping work, once again bring my eyes to the lens and continue working: for the lonely Cross is calling for a pair of shoulders to carry it."

278 Have presence of God and you will have supernatural life.

SUPERNATURAL LIFE

279 People have a plane-like vision, stuck to the earth, of two dimensions. –When you live a supernatural life, God will give you the third dimension: height, and with it, perspective, weight and volume.

280 If you lose the supernatural meaning of your life, your charity will be philanthropy; your purity, decency; your mortification, stupidity; your discipline, a whip, and all your works, barren.

281 Silence is like the doorkeeper of the interior life.

282 Paradox: Sanctity is more attainable than learning, but it's easier to be learned than to be a saint.

283 Relaxation. –You need relaxation!... opening your eyes wide so as to take in the images of things better, or almost closing them, because you're shortsighted...

Close them altogether!: have interior life, and you will see, in undreamt-of relief and colour, the wonders of a better world, of a new world: and you will draw close to God... and recognise your wretchedness... and you will become godly... with a godliness which, in bringing you nearer to your Father, will make you more of a brother to your fellow men.

284 An aspiration: May I myself be good, and everyone else better than me.

285 Conversion is the matter of a moment. –Sanctification is the work of a lifetime.

286 There is nothing better in the world than to be in the grace of God.

287 Purity of intention. –You will have it always if, always and in everything, you seek only to please God.

288 Enter into the Wounds of Christ Crucified. –There you will learn to guard your senses, you will have interior life, and you will continually offer to the Father the sufferings of Our Lord and those of Mary, in payment of your debts and of all the debts of mankind.

289 Your holy impatience, to serve him, does not displease God. –But it will prove fruitless if it is not accompanied by a real improvement in your daily conduct.

290 To rectify. –A little each day. –This must be your constant task if you really want to become a saint.

291 You have an obligation to sanctify yourself. –Yes, you too. –Who thinks that this task is only for priests and religious?

To everyone, without exception, Our Lord said: "Be perfect, as my Heavenly Father is perfect."

292 Your interior life has to be just that: to begin... and to begin again.

293 In your interior life, have you considered, slowly, the beauty of "serving" with real, present, willingness?

294 The plants could not be seen, as they lay hidden under the snow. –And the farmer who owned the land observed with satisfaction: "Now they are growing on the inside."

–I thought of you: of your forced inactivity...

–Tell me: are you too growing on the inside?

295 If you are not master of yourself, even though you may be powerful, your mastery moves me to nothing but pity and laughter.

296 It is painful to read, in the Holy Gospels, that question of Pilate's: "Whom do you wish me to release to you, Barabbas or Jesus, who is called Christ?" –It's even harder to hear the reply: "Barabbas!"

And it is more frightening still to realise that, very often!, by going astray, I too have said "Barabbas!", and I've added

"Christ?... *Crucifige eum!* – Crucify him!"

297 All that, which is worrying you at present, is of relative importance. –What is of absolute importance is that you be happy, that you be saved.

298 New lights! –What joy you have because God has made you discover a new Mediterranean!

–Make the most of those moments: now's the time to break into a hymn of thanksgiving: and it's also the time to clean up odd corners of your soul, to get out of some rut, to act more supernaturally, to avoid giving possible scandal to your neighbour...

–In a word: let your gratitude show itself in a concrete resolution.

299 Christ has died for you. –You... what should you do for Christ?

300 Your personal experience – that distaste, that restlessness, that bitterness – makes you sense the truth of those words of Jesus: No one can serve two masters!

MORE ABOUT INTERIOR LIFE

301 A secret. –An open secret: these world crises are crises of saints.

–God wants a handful of men "of his own" in each human activity. –And then... *pax Christi in regno Christi* – the peace of Christ in the kingdom of Christ.

302 Your Crucifix. –As a Christian, you should always carry your Crucifix with you. And place it on your work table. And kiss it before you go to rest and when you awake: and when your poor body rebels against your soul, kiss it again.

303 Lose that fear of calling the Lord by his name – Jesus – and of telling him that you love him.

304 Each day try to find some minutes of that blessed solitude which you so much need to keep your interior life going.

305 You wrote to me: "Simplicity is like the salt of perfection. And it's what I lack. I want to acquire it, with His help and yours."

–Neither His nor mine will be lacking. –Use the means.

306 That man's life on earth is warfare, is something that Job said many centuries ago.

–There are still some easygoing individuals who haven't got the message.

307 That supernatural mode of conduct is a truly military tactic. –You carry on the war – the daily struggles of your interior life – in positions that you have placed far from the main walls of your fortress.

And the enemy goes there: to a little mortification of yours, to your regular prayer, to your methodical work, to your plan of life: and with difficulty will he reach the easily assailed battlements of your castle. –And, if he does, he will arrive exhausted.

308 You've written to me and I quote: "My joy and my peace. I can never have real happiness if I don't have peace. And what is peace? Peace is something closely related to war. Peace is a consequence of victory. Peace demands of me a continuous struggle. Without struggle I won't be able to have peace."

309 See what depths of mercy are found in God's justice! –For in human law courts, he who pleads guilty is punished, but in God's, he is pardoned.

Blessed be the holy Sacrament of Penance!

310 *Induimini Dominum Iesum Christum* – "Put on the Lord Jesus Christ", Saint Paul said to the Romans. –It is in the Sacrament of Penance that you and I put on Jesus Christ and his merits.

311 War! –"War has a supernatural purpose," you tell me, "that the world is unaware of: the war has been for us..."

–War is the greatest obstacle to the easy way. –But we shall, in the end, have to love it, as the religious should love his disciplines.

312 The power of your name, Lord! –I headed my letter, as I usually do, "May Jesus watch over you for me".

–And they reply: "That 'May Jesus watch over you for me!' in your letter has already helped me out of one tight corner. May He also watch over all of you."

313 "Since Our Lord is helping me with his usual generosity, I will try to respond by being more 'considerate' in my ways," you told me. –And I had nothing to add.

314 I wrote to you, and was saying to you: "I'm relying on you: you must work out what we can do...!" –What could we do, but find our support in Him!

315 A missionary. –You dream of being

a missionary. You feel the fervour of a Francis Xavier: and you long to conquer for Christ an empire. –Japan, China, India, Russia..., the cold countries in the North of Europe, or America, or Africa, or Australia?

–Keep those fires going in your heart, that hunger for souls. But don't forget that you're more of a missionary by "obeying". Geographically distant from those apostolic fields, you are working both "here" and "there": don't you feel – like Francis Xavier! – your arm tired after administering baptism to so many!

316 You tell me, "Yes", that you want to. –Fine, but... do you want to as a miser cherishes his gold, as a mother loves her child, as a man of ambition craves for honours or as a wretched sensualist seeks his pleasure?

–No? –Then, you don't want to.

317 What zeal men put into their earthly affairs!: dreaming of honours, striving for riches, bent on sensuality. –Men and women, rich and poor, old and middle-aged and young and even children: all of them the same.

–When you and I put the same zeal into the affairs of our soul we will have a living and operative faith: and there will be no obstacle that we cannot overcome in our apostolic undertakings.

318 For you, who like sports, what a good argument is this one that the Apostle used!: *Nescitis quod ii qui in stadio currunt omnes quidem currunt, sed unus accipit bravium? Sic currite ut comprehendatis.* "Do you not know that of those who run in the race, though all indeed run, only one gains the prize? Run then in such a way as to win it."

319 Recollect yourself. –Seek God within you and listen to him.

320 Foster those noble thoughts, those holy desires which are awakening in you... –A single spark can start a conflagration.

321 Apostolic soul: doesn't that intimacy of Jesus with you, so close to Him, for so many years!, say anything to you?

322 It's true that I always call our Tabernacle Bethany... –Make friends with the Master's friends: Lazarus, Martha, Mary. –And then you will no longer ask me why I call our Tabernacle Bethany.

323 You know that there are "evangelical counsels". To follow them is a refinement of Love. –They say that it is a way for the few. –At times, I think it could be a way for many.

324 *Quia hic homo coepit aedificare et non potuit consummare!* – he began to build and was not able to finish!

A sad commentary, which, if you don't want it, will not be made about you: for you have all the means to crown the edifice of your sanctification: the grace of God and your own will.

LUKEWARMNESS

325 Fight against that feebleness which makes you lazy and careless in your spiritual life. –Remember that it can be the beginning of lukewarmness..., and, in the words of Scripture, God will vomit the lukewarm out of his mouth.

326 It grieves me to see the danger of lukewarmness in which you find yourself when I don't see you going seriously for perfection within your state in life.

–Say with me: I don't want lukewarmness!: *Confige timore tuo carnes meas!* –Grant me, my God, a filial fear which will make me react!

327 Yes, I know that you avoid mortal

sins. –You want to be saved! –But you are not worried about continually and deliberately falling into venial sins, even though you feel God's call, to conquer yourself each time.

–It is your lukewarmness that makes you have that bad will.

328 How little Love of God you have when you give in without a fight, just because it is not a grave sin!

329 Venial sins do a lot of harm to the soul. –Therefore, *Capite nobis vulpes parvulas, quae demoliuntur vineas,* God says in the Canticle of Canticles: Catch the little foxes that destroy the vine.

330 How sad you make me as long as you don't feel sorrow for your venial sins! –For, until then, you will not have begun to have real interior life.

331 You are lukewarm if you carry out lazily and reluctantly the things that have to do with Our Lord; if calculatingly or "craftily" you look for ways of cutting down your duties; if you think only of yourself and of your comfort; if your conversations are idle and vain; if you don't abhor venial sin; if you act from human motives.

STUDY

332 When a person can become learned we cannot excuse him if he does not.

333 Study. –Obedience: *non multa, sed multum* – not many things, but much.

334 You pray, you mortify yourself, you work in a thousand apostolic activities..., but you do not study. –You are no use then if you don't change.

Study, professional formation of whatever type it be, is a serious obligation among us.

335 An hour of study, for a modern apostle, is an hour of prayer.

336 If you are to serve God with your mind, for you study is a serious obligation.

337 You frequent the Sacraments, you pray, you are chaste... but you do not study. –Don't tell me you're good: you're only "goodish".

338 Formerly, since human knowledge – science – was very limited, it seemed quite feasible for a single learned individual to undertake the defence and apologia of our Holy Faith.

Today, with the extension and intensity of modern science, the apologists have to divide the work among them in order to defend the Church scientifically in all fields.

–You... cannot shirk this obligation.

339 Books: don't buy them without getting advice from Christians who have knowledge and discernment. –You could be buying something useless or harmful.

How often people think they've got a book under their arm... and it turns out to be a load of filth!

340 Study. –Study in earnest. –If you are to be salt and light, you need knowledge, and suitable training.

Or do you imagine that an idle and lazy life will entitle you to receive infused knowledge?

341 It is good to see you put such determination into your study, always provided you put the same determination into acquiring interior life.

342 Don't forget that before teaching one must do. –*Coepit facere et docere,* Holy Scripture says of Jesus Christ: "He began to do and to teach."

–The "doing" came first. So that you and I might learn.

343 Get working. –When you have the responsibility of a professional job, the life of your soul will improve: and you will become more of a man, because you'll get rid of that habit of "picking holes" in everything.

344 Teacher: your keenness to know and

practise the best methods of helping your students to acquire earthly knowledge is undeniable. But be equally keen to know and practise Christian asceticism, which is the only method of helping them and yourself to be better.

345 Culture, culture! –Very good: let us be second to none in striving for it and possessing it.

–But, culture is a means and not an end.

346 Student: train yourself in a solid and active piety, excel in study, have firm desires of doing apostolate in your profession. –And, on the strength of your religious and scientific training, I promise you rapid and far-reaching developments.

347 You're only concerned about building up your knowledge. –And it's necessary to build up your soul. –Then you will work as you ought, for Christ: for Him to reign in the world there is need of people who, with their eyes fixed on heaven, will work with dedication and distinction in all human activities and, from them, carry out quietly – and effectively – an apostolate of a professional nature.

348 Your indolence, your half-heartedness, your laziness, are cowardice and comfort-seeking – as your conscience constantly keeps telling you – but “they are not the way”.

349 You shouldn’t worry if what you stated was an orthodox opinion, even though the malice of the person listening to you led him to be scandalised. –Because his scandal is pharisaical.

350 It’s not enough to be learned, as well as being a good Christian. –If you don’t correct the brusqueness of your character, if you make your zeal and your knowledge incompatible with good manners, I don’t see how you can become a saint. –And, if you are learned, even though you are, you deserve to be tethered to a manger, like a mule.

351 With that self-satisfied air you’re becoming an annoying and disagreeable sort of person, you're making a fool of yourself and, what's worse, you're lessening the effectiveness of your work as an apostle.

Don't forget that even "mediocrities" can sin by being pompous.

352 Your very inexperience leads you to that presumption, to that vanity, to that which you imagine gives you an air of importance.

–Please correct your behaviour. Foolish and all, you may come to occupy a position of responsibility (it has happened more than once) and, if you are not convinced of your lack of qualities, you will refuse to listen to those who have the gift of counsel. –And it's frightening to think of the harm your mismanagement will do.

353 Non-denominationalism. Neutrality. –Old myths always trying to appear new.

Have you ever stopped to think how absurd it is to leave one's Catholicism aside on entering university or a professional association, a learned society or parliament, like a man leaving his hat at the door?

354 I want you to make good use of your time. –Don't forget the fig tree cursed by Our Lord. And it was doing something: sprouting leaves. Like you...

–Don't tell me you have excuses. –It was of no avail to the fig tree, the Evangelist tells us, that it was not the time for figs, when Our Lord went to it looking for them.

–And barren it remained for ever.

355 People engaged in human business say that time is money. –That's not saying much, in my opinion: for us who are engaged in the business of souls, time is... glory!

356 I don't see how you can call yourself a Christian and lead such an aimless, useless life. –Have you forgotten Christ's life of toil?

357 "All the sins," you told me, "seem to be just waiting for the first moment of

idleness. Why, idleness itself must be a sin!"

–A person who has committed himself to work for Christ should never have a free moment, because to rest is not to do nothing: it is to relax in activities which require less effort.

358 To be idle is something that doesn't make sense in a man with an apostolic soul.

359 Put a supernatural motive behind your ordinary professional work, and you will have sanctified your work.

FORMATION

360 How frankly you laughed when I advised you to put the years of your youth under the protection of Saint Raphael!: "So that he'll lead you to a holy marriage, as he did with young Tobias, with a woman who is good and pretty and rich" I told you, jokingly.

And then, how thoughtful you became! when I carried on and advised you to put yourself also under the patronage of that youthful apostle, John: in case Our Lord was asking more of you.

361 For you, who complain inwardly, because you're harshly treated, and you feel the contrast between this harshness and the way you're treated by your own family, I copy these lines from the letter of an army

doctor: "With the sick, you can have the conscientious professional approach, cold and calculating, but objective and useful to the patient, or you can have the tearful fussing of a family. –What would become of a first-aid post, at the height of a battle, when the stream of casualties begins to arrive and to build up because they can't be dealt with fast enough, if around each stretcher there was a family? One would almost feel like going over to the enemy."

362 I don't need miracles: I have more than enough with those in Scripture. –On the other hand, I do need your fulfilment of your duty, your response to grace.

363 Disappointed. –You arrive downhearted. For men have just taught you a lesson! –As long as they thought you did not need them, they were full of offers of help. But the possibility that they might have to help you financially – a few miserable pennies – turned their friendship into indifference.

–Trust only in God and in those who, through Him, are united to you.

364 Ah, if only you would resolve to serve God "seriously", with the same zeal with which you serve your ambition, your vanities, your sensuality!...

365 If you feel an impulse to be a leader, your aim should be this: among your brothers, to be the last; among others, the first.

366 Let's see: what offence is done to you because this person or that gets on better with someone else, whom they knew before or for whom they feel greater affinity, by temperament, profession or character?

–Nevertheless, among your own people, carefully avoid even the appearance of a particular friendship.

367 The choicest, finest delicacy, if eaten by a pig (to put it bluntly) turns, at best,... into pig's flesh!

Let us be angels, so as to dignify the ideas we assimilate. –Or else, let us be men: so as to convert the food we eat, at least, into fine and noble muscles, or perhaps into a powerful brain... capable of understanding and adoring God.

–But... let us not be animals, like so many, so very many!

368 So you are bored? –It's because you keep your senses awake and your soul asleep.

369 The charity of Jesus Christ will lead you to make concessions many times... and very nobly. –And the charity of Jesus Christ will lead you to be intransigent many times... very nobly as well.

370 If you are not bad, and yet appear to be, then you are stupid. –And that stupidity – a source of scandal – is worse than being bad.

371 When you see people of doubtful professional reputation buzzing about and taking a prominent part in outward shows of religiosity, don't you feel the urge to whisper in their ears: Please, would you mind being just a little less Catholic!

372 If you have an official position, you also have certain rights, which go with it, and certain duties.

–You are straying from your path as an apostle if the occasion – or the excuse – of a work of zeal makes you leave the duties of your position undone. For you will be losing that professional prestige, which is your very “bait” as a “fisher of men”.

373 I like your apostolic motto: “To work without rest”.

374 Why that rushing around? –Don’t tell me it’s activity: it’s thoughtlessness.

375 Dissipation. –You let your senses and faculties slake their thirst in any pool you find. –And afterwards see how you are: unsettled, your attention scattered, your will asleep and your concupiscence awake.

–Subject yourself seriously once again to a plan that will make you lead a Christian life, or you’ll never do anything worthwhile.

376 “What an influence the environment

has!" you told me. –And I had to answer: Quite. That's why your formation has to be such that you take your own environment with you, in a natural manner, so as to give "your tone" to the society in which you live.

–And then, if you have grasped this spirit, I'm sure you'll tell me, with all the amazement of the early disciples as they contemplated the first-fruits of the miracles being worked by their hands in Christ's name: "What an influence we have on the environment!"

377 And how shall I acquire "our formation", and how shall I keep "our spirit"? –By fulfilling the specific norms your Director gave you and explained to you and taught you to love: fulfil them and you will be an apostle.

378 Don't be a pessimist. –Don't you realise that everything that happens or can happen is for the good?

–Your optimism will be a necessary consequence of your faith.

379 Naturalness. –Let your lives as Christian gentlemen, as Christian women – your salt and your light – flow spontaneously, without anything odd or silly: carry our spirit of simplicity with you always.

380 "And in a paganised or pagan environment, when the atmosphere clashes with my life, won't my naturalness seem artificial?" you ask me.

–And I reply: Undoubtedly your life will clash with theirs: and that contrast, because you're confirming your faith with deeds, is exactly the naturalness I want of you.

381 Don't worry if people say you have "esprit de corps". What do they want? A feeble instrument, that falls apart the moment it is grasped?

382 When I made you a present of that Life of Jesus, I wrote in it this inscription: "May you seek Christ: May you find Christ: May you love Christ."

–They are three perfectly clear stages. Have you tried, at least, to live the first?

383 If they see you weaken... and you are the leader, it is no wonder their obedience falters.

384 Muddled thinking. –It came to my knowledge that your soundness of judgement was faltering. And, to help you understand me, I wrote to you: The devil has a very ugly face and, since he's so clever, he won't risk our seeing his horns. He doesn't make frontal attacks.

–That's why he so often comes in the disguise of nobleness and even of spirituality!

385 Our Lord says: "A new commandment I give you: to love one another. By this will men know you are my disciples."

–And Saint Paul: "Bear each other's burdens, and so you shall fulfil the law of Christ."

–I have nothing to add.

386 Do not forget, my son, that for you in this world there is but one evil, which you must fear, and avoid with the grace of God: sin.

THE PLANE OF YOUR SANCTITY

387 The plane of sanctity that God expects of us is determined by these three points:

Holy intransigence, holy coercion and holy shamelessness.

388 Holy shamelessness is one thing, lay cheekiness quite another.

389 Holy shamelessness is a characteristic of the "life of childhood". A little child worries about nothing. –His weak points, his natural weak points, show up quite simply, even if everyone is watching...

This shamelessness, applied to the supernatural life, brings with it the following train of reasoning: praise, contempt...:

admiration, ridicule...: honour, dishonour...: health, sickness...: wealth, poverty...: beauty, ugliness...

All right;... who cares?

390 Laugh at ridicule. –Despise the fear of what people may say. See and feel God in your own self and in your surroundings. –That way you will end up acquiring the holy shamelessness that you need, what a paradox!, in order to live with the refinement of a Christian gentleman.

391 If you have holy shamelessness, why care about "what have people said" or "what will people say"?

392 Convince yourself that there is no such thing as ridicule for whoever is doing what is best.

393 A man, a... gentleman ready to compromise, would condemn Jesus to death again.

394 Readiness to compromise is a sure sign of not possessing the truth. –When a man makes concessions in matters of ideals, of honour or of Faith, that man is a... man without ideals, without honour and without Faith.

395 That man of God, an old campaigner, reasoned as follows: “So I won’t yield an inch? Of course not!: because I’m convinced my ideal is true. You, on the other hand, are very ready to compromise...: Would you agree that two and two make three and a half? –No?... Not even for friendship’s sake will you yield in such a tiny thing?

–That’s because, for the first time, you are convinced you’ve got the truth... and you’ve come over to my side!”

396 Holy intransigence is not intemperance.

397 Be uncompromising in doctrine and in conduct. –But be gentle in manner. –A powerful steel mace, wrapped in a quilted covering.

–Be uncompromising, but don’t be pig-headed.

398 Intransigence is not just simply intransigence: it is “holy intransigence”.

Let’s not forget that there is also a “holy coercion”.

399 If, to save an earthly life, we can, with the applause of everyone, use force to prevent someone from committing suicide... are we not allowed to use the same coercion – holy coercion – to save the Life (with a capital letter) of many who are stupidly bent on killing their souls?

400 How many crimes are committed in the name of justice! –If you were a dealer in fire-arms and someone offered you the price of one of them, so as to use that weapon to kill your mother, would you sell it to him?... Yet, wasn’t he ready to pay you a fair price for it?...

–Professor, journalist, politician, diplomat: reflect.

401 God and daring! –Daring is not imprudence. –Daring is not bravado.

402 Don’t ask Jesus for pardon just for

your own faults: don't love him just with your own heart...

Make up to him for all the offences that have been done to him, are being done to him and will be done to him... Love him with all the strength of all the hearts of all those who have loved him most.

Be daring: tell him that you are crazier about him than Mary Magdalen, than Teresa and little Thérèse..., that you are more madly in love with him than Augustine and Dominic and Francis, more than Ignatius and Francis Xavier.

403 Be more daring still and, when you need something, while keeping always true to the *Fiat,* don't ask: say "Jesus, I want this or that", for that's the way children ask.

404 You've failed! –We never fail. –You put all your trust in God. –After that, you did not neglect any human means.

Convince yourself of this fact: your success – this time, in this – was to fail. –Give thanks to God and... begin again!

405 Have you failed? –You – you're utterly convinced – cannot fail.

You haven't failed: you've gained experience. –On you go!

406 That was a failure, a disaster: because you lost our spirit. –You know well that, if we look at things supernaturally, the outcome (victory? defeat? who cares!) has only one name: Success.

407 Let's not confuse the rights of the office one holds with personal rights. –The former cannot be renounced.

408 Sanctimoniousness is to sanctity, what affected devotion is to true piety: its caricature.

409 We must remember that our apparently saintly virtue is of no value unless it goes hand in hand with the ordinary virtues of a Christian.

–That would be like adorning oneself with splendid jewels over one's underwear.

410 Let not your virtue be a noisy virtue.

411 Many false apostles, in spite of themselves, do good to the crowd, to the people, through the very power of the doctrine of Jesus which they preach, even though they don't practise it.

But this good does not make up for the enormous, practical harm they do by killing the souls of leaders, of apostles, who turn away, disgusted, from those who do not practise what they teach others to do.

That is why, if men or women are not willing to lead an upright life, they should never put themselves in the front line, as leaders of a group.

412 May the fire of your Love not be a will-o'-the-wisp – an illusion, a deceitful fire, that neither sets ablaze what it touches, nor gives any heat.

413 The *Non serviam,* "I will not serve", of Satan has been too fruitful. –Do you not feel a generous urge to say each day, with a willingness to pray and work, a *Serviam* – I will serve you! I will be faithful to you! – which will surpass in fruitfulness that cry of revolt?

414 How pitiful is a "man of God" who has fallen away! –But how much more pitiful is a "man of God" who is lukewarm and worldly!

415 Pay little heed to what the world calls victories or defeats. –So often the victor comes out defeated!

416 *Sine me nihil potestis facere!* "Without me you can do nothing!" New light, or rather, new splendour, for my eyes, from that Eternal Light, which the Holy Gospel is.

–Now can I be surprised by "my"... silly mistakes?

–Let me bring Jesus into all my things. And, then, there will be no silly mistakes in my conduct: and, if I am to speak accurately, I will no longer say my things, but "our things".

LOVE OF GOD

417 There is no other love than Love!

418 The secret to give a true value to the humblest, even the most humiliating thing, is to love.

419 –A Child. –A Sick Person. –As you write these words, don't you feel tempted to put them with a capital letter?

It's because, for a soul in love, children and sick people are He.

420 How little a life is to offer to God!...

421 A friend is a treasure. –So then... *a* Friend!..., for where your treasure is, there is your heart.

422 Jesus is your friend. –The Friend. –With a heart of flesh, like yours. –With eyes, which look so lovingly, which wept for Lazarus...

–And as much as he loves Lazarus, he loves you.

423 My God, I love you, but... teach me how to love!

424 Chastise for Love's sake: this is the secret of how to raise to a supernatural plane the punishment imposed on those who deserve it.

For the love of God, who has been offended, let the punishment serve as reparation. For the love of our neighbour through God, let the punishment serve, never as a vengeance, but as a healing medicine.

425 To know that you love me so much, my God, and... I haven't gone crazy!

426 In Christ we have every ideal: for he is King, he is Love, he is God.

427 Lord: may I have due measure in everything... except in Love.

428 If Love, even human love, gives so many consolations here, what will Love be like in heaven?

429 Everything that is done for Love acquires beauty and becomes great.

430 Jesus, may I be last in everything... and first in Love.

431 Do not fear God's Justice. –In God, as admirable and lovable is his Justice as his Mercy: both are proofs of Love.

432 Consider what is most beautiful and most noble on earth..., what pleases the mind and the other faculties..., and what delights the flesh and the senses...

And the world, and the other worlds, that shine in the night: the whole Universe. –Well this, along with all the follies of the heart satisfied..., is worth nothing, is nothing and less than nothing, beside... this God of mine! – of yours! –, this infinite treasure, most beautiful pearl, humbled, become a slave, lowered to nothingness in the form of a servant in the stable where he chose to be born, in Joseph's workshop, in his Passion and in his ignominious death... and in the madness of Love which is the Blessed Eucharist.

433 Live by Love and you will conquer always – even though you be defeated – in the Navas* and Lepantos• of your interior struggle.

434 Let your heart overflow in effusions of Love and gratitude as you consider how God's grace saves you each day from the snares the enemy sets in your path.

435 *Timor Domini sanctus.* –Holy is the fear of God. –A fear which is a son's veneration for his Father, never a servile fear,

---

* Las Navas de Tolosa: location, in southern Spain, of the famous battle of 1212 won by the armies of the Christian kingdoms of the Iberian peninsula over the Muslims of Andalusia and northern Africa. –Trans.

• Lepanto: naval battle fought off the coast of Greece in 1571 between Turkish and Christian squadrons, and won by the Christian fleet. –Trans.

because your Father-God is not a tyrant.

436 Love-sorrow. –Because He is good. –Because he's your Friend, who gave his Life for you. –Because all the good you have is his. –Because you have offended him so much... Because he has forgiven you... He!... you!!

–Weep, my son, with Love-sorrow.

437 If a man had died to save me from death!...

–God died. And I remain indifferent.

438 Crazy! –I saw you – alone, so you thought, in the bishop's chapel – leaving a kiss on each newly-consecrated chalice and paten: so that He might find it there, when he "came down" for the first time to those eucharistic vessels.

439 Don't forget that Sorrow is the touchstone of Love.

CHARITY

440 When you have finished your work, do your brother's, helping him, for love of Christ, so tactfully and so naturally that not even the person you're helping realises that you are doing more than in justice you ought.

–This indeed is virtue befitting a son of God!

441 You are hurt by your neighbour's lack of charity towards you. How much God must be hurt by your lack of charity, of Love, towards Him!

442 Don't allow yourself to think badly of anyone, even though the words or actions of the person in question give you reasonable grounds for doing so.

443 Don't make negative criticism: when you can't praise, say nothing.

444 Never speak badly of your brother, even though you may have more than enough reasons for doing so. –Go first to the Tabernacle, and then go to the Priest, your father, and open your heart to him too about your worry.

–And to no one else.

445 Gossip is grime that soils and obstructs the apostolate. –It goes against charity, it saps energy, takes away peace, and destroys one's union with God.

446 If you are so wretched, why are you surprised that others have some wretchedness?

447 After seeing how many, entire!, lives are spent (tongues wagging, wagging, wagging, with all the consequences), I feel a greater need and a greater love for silence. –And I well understand, Lord, why you will ask us to account for our idle words.

448 It's easier said than done. –You... who have that cutting, hatchet-like, tongue, have you tried even once, even by chance, to do "well" what, according to your "considered" opinion, others do less well?

449 That should be called: mumbling, murmuring, mischief-making, intrigue, gossip, tale-bearing, plotting... slander?, vileness?

–It is difficult for the "sitting in judgement", by those who have no call to judge, not to end up as "old maids' gossip".

450 How much God is hurt and how much harm is done to many souls – and how much others can be sanctified – by the injustice of the "just"!

451 Let us not wish to judge. –Each one sees things from his own point of view... and with his own understanding, which almost always is quite limited, and through eyes that are often dimmed and clouded by passion.

Moreover, as happens with those modernist painters, the outlook of certain people is so subjective and so sickly, that they dash off a few random strokes and assure us that they represent our portrait, our conduct...

Of what little worth are the judgements of men! –Don't judge without sifting your judgement in prayer.

452 Make an effort, if necessary, always to forgive those who offend you, from the very first moment, for, no matter how great the injury or offence that has been done to you, God has forgiven you more.

453 Do you speak badly of others? –Then you are losing the right spirit and, if you don't learn to check your tongue, each word will take you one step nearer the exit from that apostolic undertaking in which you work.

454 Do not judge without hearing both sides. –It can very easily happen, even with people who think themselves virtuous, that they forget this elementary rule of prudence.

455 Do you know what damage you can cause by hurling a stone with your eyes blindfold?

–Neither do you know the harm you can do, at times it could be serious, by throwing out uncharitable remarks that to you seem trifling, because your eyes are blinded by thoughtlessness or passion.

456 To criticise, to destroy, is not difficult: even the rawest labourer can drive his pick into the noble and finely-hewn stone of a cathedral.

–To construct: that is what requires the skill of a master.

457 Who are you to judge whether the superior has got things right? –Don't you see that when he judges he has more to go on than you; more experience; truer, wiser and more dispassionate advisers; and, above all, he has more grace, a special grace, the grace of state, which is a light he has and a powerful aid from God?

458 Those clashes with the world's self-ishness will make you appreciate all the more the fraternal charity of your own people.

459 Your charity is... presumptuous. –From afar, you attract: you have light. –Close to, you repel: you lack warmth. –What a pity!

460 *Frater qui adiuvatur a fratre quasi civitas firma* –A brother helped by his brother is as strong as a walled city.

–Think a while and make up your mind to live the fraternal spirit I've always recommended to you.

461 If I don't see you practise that blessed brotherly spirit that I preach to you constantly, I shall remind you of those affectionate words of Saint John: *Filioli mei, non diligamus verbo neque lingua, sed opere et veritate* –My little children, let us not love by word nor with the tongue, but in deed and in truth.

462 The power of charity! –Your mutual weakness will even be a support that keeps you upright in the fulfilment of duty if you live that blessed fraternal spirit: just as playing cards, leaning on each other, mutually support one another.

463 More than in "giving", charity consists in "understanding". –Therefore find an excuse for your neighbour, there are always excuses to be found, if it is your duty to judge.

464 You know that someone's soul is in danger? –From afar, with your life of union, you can give him effective help. –On with it, then, and don't be anxious about it.

465 That concern you feel for your brothers seems a positive thing to me: it's a proof of your mutual charity. –Try to ensure, however, that your concern does not degenerate into anxiety.

466 "As a rule, people are very ungenerous with their money" you write to me. "Plenty of talk, bubbling enthusiasm, promises and plans. –But when it comes to sacrifice, few really lend a hand. And, if they do give, it has to be with some entertainment thrown in – a dance, a raffle, a film, a show – or an announcement and subscription list in the press."

–It's a sorry picture, but it has its exceptions: may you too be one of those who, when they give alms, don't let their left hand know what their right is doing.

467 Books. –I stretched out my hand, like one of Christ's beggars, and I asked for books. Books! to nourish the Catholic, Apostolic and Roman minds of many young university students.

–I stretched out my hand, like one of Christ's beggars... but again and again I was disappointed!

–Why can't people understand, Jesus, the profound Christian charity of this alms, which is more effective than giving someone a fine loaf of bread?

468 You are far too naive. –"Few people really practise charity! –To be charitable does not consist in giving old clothes or copper pennies..."

–And you tell me about your experience and your disillusionment.

–The only thing that occurs to me is this: let us, you and I, give and give ourselves without stinginess. And we will spare those who come into contact with us your sad experience.

469 "Greet all the saints. All the saints send you greetings. To all the saints who live in Ephesus. To all the saints in Christ Jesus who are at Philippi." –What a moving name – saints! – the early Christian faithful used when addressing one another!

–Learn to treat your brothers well.

THE MEANS

470 But... what means do we have? –The same ones that Peter and Paul had, and Dominic and Francis, and Ignatius and Francis Xavier: the Crucifix and the Gospel...

–Are they insufficient for you?

471 In apostolic undertakings it's a good thing, it's a duty, to consider your material means (2 + 2 = 4), but don't forget ever! that your calculations, fortunately, must include another term: God + 2 + 2...

472 Serve your God honestly, be faithful to him... and don't worry about anything: for it's a great truth that "If you seek the kingdom of God and his justice, He will give you the rest – material things, the means – in addition."

473 Cast away that despair produced by the realisation of your wretchedness. –True: in financial prestige, you are a zero..., in social standing, another zero..., and another in virtues, and another in talent...

But, to the left of these zeros, stands Christ... And what an incalculable figure we get!

474 So you are... a nobody. –And others have done wonders and are still doing them, in organisation, in the press, in publicity. –And they have all the means, while you have none?... Fine: just remember Ignatius:

Ignorant, among the doctors at Alcalá. –Poor, penniless, among the students of Paris. –Persecuted, slandered...

This is the way: love and believe and... suffer! Your Love and your Faith and your Cross are the infallible means to give effect, eternal effect, to the longings for apostolate that you bear in your heart.

475 You see yourself wretched. And that

is what you are. –In spite of that – rather, because of that – God has sought you out.

–He always uses inadequate instruments: so that it can be seen that the "work" is his.

–Of you he only asks docility.

476 When you "surrender yourself" to God there will be no difficulty that can shake your optimism.

477 Why do you allow those corners of your heart to remain ungiven? –As long as you don't give yourself completely, it's useless to try to try to take someone else to him.

–A poor instrument are you.

478 But surely you don't mean to tell me, at this stage!, that you need the approval, the warm support, the encouragement of the powerful, to go on doing what God wants?

–The powerful tend to be changeable, while you have to be constant. Be grateful, if they help you. But go ahead, unperturbed, if they despise you.

479 Take no notice. –The "prudent" have always called the works of God madness.

–Onward! Be daring!

480 Do you see? One strand and another and many, tightly twined, form that stout rope strong enough to lift enormous weights.

–You and your brothers, your wills united to carry out God's, will be capable of overcoming all obstacles.

481 When one is seeking God alone, one can rightly put into practice, in order to carry out works of zeal, a principle laid down by a good friend of ours: "Spend what you ought, though you owe all you spend."

482 What does it matter if you have the whole world with all its powers against you? You... keep going!

–Repeat the words of the Psalm: "The Lord is my light and my salvation, whom shall I fear?... *Si consistant adversum me castra, non timebit cor meum.* Even if I should see myself surrounded by enemies, my heart will not weaken."

483 Courage! You... *can!* –Don't you see what God's grace did with that dozing, denying, cowardly Peter?... with that persecuting, hating, obstinate Paul?

484 Be an instrument: of gold or steel, of platinum or iron... large or small, delicate or rough...

–Every one is useful: each has his own mission. As in material things: would anyone dare to assert that the carpenter's saw is less useful than the surgeon's forceps?

–Your duty is to be an instrument.

485 All right. But what does it matter? –I can't understand why you think of withdrawing from that work with souls (unless it's through hidden pride: you think yourself perfect), just because God's fire, which attracted you, as well as giving the light and warmth that fill you with enthusiasm, at times also produces some smoke due to the weakness of the instruments.

486 Work... there's plenty to be done. –The instruments mustn't be left to grow rusty. –And there are standard procedures

to avoid mildew and rust. –Just put them into practice.

487 Don't lose sleep over the financial difficulties that are coming upon your apostolic undertaking. –Increase your trust in God, do all you humanly can, and you'll see how soon money ceases to be a difficulty!

488 Don't put off doing things because you haven't the instruments: one begins as best one can. –With time, the function creates the organ. Some, that were no use, turn out to be suitable. The rest are put through a surgical operation, a painful one perhaps – the saints were wonderful "surgeons"! – and so the work carries on.

489 A keen, living faith. A faith like Peter's. –When you have it – the Lord himself has said so – you will move mountains, the humanly insuperable obstacles that stand in the way of your apostolic undertakings.

490 An upright heart and good will: with these two components and your eye intent on carrying out what God wants, you will see your dreams of Love come true and your hunger for souls satisfied.

491 *Nonne hic est fabri filius? Nonne hic est faber, filius Mariae?* Is this not the craftsman's son? Is this not the craftsman, the son of Mary?

–This was said of Jesus and may very well be said of you, in a tone half of astonishment, half mocking, when you decide *once and for all* to carry out God's Will, to be an instrument: "But, isn't this so-and-so...?"

–Say nothing. And let your works confirm your mission.

OUR LADY

492 Love for our Mother will be the breath that kindles into a living flame the embers of virtue hidden among the ashes of your lukewarmness.

493 Love Our Lady. And She will obtain for you abundant grace to conquer in this daily struggle. –And the evil one will gain nothing from those foul things, that are continually boiling and rising within you, trying to engulf with their sweet-smelling corruption the high ideals, the sublime commands that Christ himself has placed in your heart. –*Serviam!* I will serve!

494 Be Mary's and you will be ours.

495 One always goes to Jesus and one "returns" to him through Mary.

496 How people like to be reminded of their relationship with distinguished figures in literature, in politics, in the services, in the Church!...

–Sing to Mary Immaculate, reminding her:

Hail Mary, daughter of God the Father; Hail Mary, Mother of God the Son; Hail Mary, Spouse of God the Holy Spirit... Greater than thou, none but God!

497 Say: Mother of mine – yours, because you are hers on many counts – may your love bind me to your Son's Cross: may I not lack Faith, or courage, or daring, to carry out the will of our Jesus.

498 All the sins of your life seem to be rising up against you. –Don't lose heart. –Rather, call on your Mother, Holy Mary, with the faith and abandonment of a child. She will bring peace to your soul.

499 Mary most Holy, Mother of God,

passes unnoticed, as just one more among the women of her village.

–Learn from her how to live with "naturalness".

500 Wear on your breast the holy scapular of Carmel. –Few devotions – and there are many very fine Marian devotions – are so deep-rooted among the faithful and so richly blessed by the Popes. –Besides, how motherly this sabbatine privilege is!

501 When you were asked what picture of Our Lady aroused your devotion most, and you answered – like someone with long experience – "All of them", I realised that you were a good son: that's why you like – "They make me fall in love", you said – all the pictures of your Mother.

502 Mary, Teacher of prayer. –See how she asks her Son, at Cana. And how she insists, without losing heart, with perseverance. –And how she succeeds.

–Learn.

503 The loneliness of Mary. Alone! –She

weeps, forsakenly.

–You and I should keep Our Lady company, and weep also: for Jesus has been fastened to the wood, with nails, our miseries.

504 The Holy Virgin Mary, Mother of Fair Love, will quieten your heart, when it makes you feel that it is of flesh, if you have recourse to Her with confidence.

505 Love for Our Lady is proof of good spirit, in organisations and in individual people.

–Distrust any undertaking that does not have this sign.

506 Our Lady of Sorrows. When you contemplate her, look into her Heart: she is a Mother with two sons, facing each other: He... and you.

507 The humility of my Mother Holy Mary! –You won't see her amid the palms of Jerusalem, nor, apart from the first-fruits of Cana, at the hour of the great miracles.

–But she doesn't flee from the

contempt of Golgotha: there, *iuxta crucem Iesu,* beside the cross of Jesus, stands his Mother.

508 Marvel at Mary's steadfastness: at the foot of the Cross, with the greatest of human sorrows – there is no sorrow like her sorrow – filled with fortitude.

–And ask her for some of that steadfastness, so that you too may know how to stand beside the Cross.

509 Mary, Teacher of hidden and silent sacrifice!

–See her, nearly always in the background, cooperating with her Son: she knows, yet says nothing.

510 You see how simply it was done? –*Ecce ancilla!...,* "Behold the handmaid..." –And the Word was made flesh.

–That's how the saints worked: without spectacle. If there was any, it was in spite of them.

511 *Ne timeas, Maria!* –Fear not, Mary!... –Our Lady was troubled at the presence of the Archangel.

–Just in case I was thinking of throwing overboard those details of modesty, that are the safeguard of my purity!

512 Oh Mother, Mother!: with that word of yours – *Fiat,* "Be it done" – you have made us brothers of God and heirs to his glory. –Bless you!

513 Before, alone, you couldn't... –Now, you have turned to Our Lady, and, with Her, how easy it is!

514 Have confidence. –Return. –Invoke Our Lady and you will be faithful.

515 So your strength is failing you? –Why don't you say so to your Mother: *Consolatrix afflictorum, Auxilium Christianorum..., Spes nostra, Regina Apostolorum* –Comfort of the afflicted, Help of Christians, Our Hope, Queen of Apostles?

516 Mother! –Call her, cry out to her. –She is listening, she sees you in danger perhaps, and she, your Mother Holy Mary, offers you, with her Son's grace, the refuge of her arms, the tenderness of her caresses: and you will find yourself with added strength for the struggle ahead.

THE CHURCH

517 *Et unam, sanctam, catholicam et apostolicam Ecclesiam!...* –I can understand why you pause, in your prayer, savouring the words: I believe in the Church, One, Holy, Catholic and Apostolic...

518 What joy, to be able to say with all the fervour of my soul: I love my Mother the holy Church!

519 That cry – *Serviam!* I will serve! – expresses a willingness to "serve" the Church of God most faithfully, even at the cost of fortune, of honour and of life.

520 Catholic, Apostolic... Roman! –I like you to be very Roman. And to long to make your "path to Rome", *videre Petrum,* to see Peter.

521 How good Christ is, to have left the Sacraments to his Church! –They are a remedy for each of our needs.

–Venerate them and be very grateful for them, to Our Lord and to his Church.

522 Have veneration and respect for the Holy Liturgy of the Church and for each of its ceremonies. –Carry them out faithfully. –Don't you see that, for us poor humans, even the greatest and most noble things must enter through the senses?

523 The Church sings, it has been said, because speech alone would not suffice for its prayer. –You, who are a Christian, and a chosen Christian, should learn to sing liturgically.

524 "Let's burst into song!" said a soul in love, after seeing the wonders that Our Lord was working through his ministry.

–And the same advice I give to you: Sing! Let your grateful enthusiasm for your

God overflow into joyful harmonies.

525 To be “Catholic” means to love one’s Country, letting no one surpass us in that love. And, at the same time, to hold as mine the noble aspirations of all countries. How many glories of France are glories of mine! And, in the same way, many things that are a matter of pride for Germans, Italians, Englishmen..., for Americans and Asians and Africans, are a source of pride for me as well.

–Catholic!: big heart, wide-open mind.

526 If you don’t have the highest reverence for the priesthood and the religious state, it isn’t true that you love the Church of God.

527 That woman who, in the house of Simon the leper, in Bethany, anoints the head of the Master with precious perfume, reminds us of our duty to be splendid in our worship of God.

–All lavishness, majesty and beauty seem little to me.

–And against those who attack the richness of sacred vessels, vestments and altarpieces, we hear the praise given by Jesus: *Opus enim bonum operata est in me* –She has done a good deed to me.

HOLY MASS

528 A very important characteristic of the apostolic man is to love the Mass.

529 The Mass is long, you say, and I add: Because your love is short.

530 Isn't it strange how many Christians, who are quite leisurely and even solemn in their social life (they are in no hurry), in the unhasty rhythm of their professional affairs, at table and in their recreation (no hurry here either), feel rushed and want to rush the Priest, in their anxiety to shorten, to hurry the time devoted to the most Holy Sacrifice of the Altar?

531 "Treat him well for me, treat him

well!" Words, mingled with tears, of an elderly Prelate to the new Priests he had just ordained.

–Lord!: would that I had the voice and the authority to repeat that same cry in the ears and in the hearts of many, many Christians!

532 How that saintly young Priest, who was found worthy of martyrdom, wept at the foot of the altar, as he thought of a soul who had come to receive Christ in a state of mortal sin!

–Is that how you offer him reparation?

533 The humility of Jesus: in Bethlehem, in Nazareth, on Calvary... –But more humiliation and more self-abasement in the Sacred Host: more than in the stable, more than in Nazareth, more than on the Cross.

That is why I must love the Mass so much! (*Our* Mass, Jesus...)

534 Going to Communion daily for so many years! –Anybody else would be a saint by now, you told me, and I... I'm always the same!

Son, I replied, keep up your daily Communion, and think: What would I be if I had not gone?

535 Communion, union, communication, trust: Word, Bread, Love.

536 Go to Communion. –It's not disrespect. –Go this very day, when you have just got out of that snare.

–Have you forgotten that Jesus said: It is not the healthy who need the physician, but those who are sick?

537 When you approach the Tabernacle remember that He!... has been waiting for you for twenty centuries.

538 There he is: he is King of Kings, and Lord of Lords. –He is hidden in the Bread.

To this extreme has he humbled himself for love of you.

539 He has stayed here for *you.* –It's not reverence to stay away from Communion, if you are well disposed. –Irreverence you'd show only if you received him unworthily.

540 What a source of grace spiritual Communion is! –Practise it frequently and you will have more presence of God and closer union with Him in your deeds.

541 Piety has its own good manners. –Learn them. –What a pity to see those "pious" people who don't know how to attend Mass (even though they go daily), or how to make the sign of the Cross (they make weird gestures, all in a hurry), or how to bend the knee before the Tabernacle (their ridiculous genuflections seem a mockery), or how to bow their heads reverently before a picture of Our Lady.

542 Don't put up those "mass-produced" images for public devotion: I prefer a figure of Christ made of rough wrought-iron to those painted plaster Crucifixes that look as if they are made of sugar candy.

543 You saw me celebrate the Holy Mass on a bare altar – table and altar-stone – without a reredos. The Crucifix, large-size. The candlesticks solid, with thick wax candles of graded height, sloping up towards the

Cross. The frontal, of the colour of the day. A sweeping chasuble. The chalice rich, sober in lines, with a broad cup. No electric light, nor did we miss it.

–And you found it difficult to leave the oratory: one felt at home there. Do you see how we are drawn towards God, brought closer to Him, by the strictness of the liturgy?

COMMUNION OF SAINTS

544 Communion of Saints. –How shall I explain it? –You see what blood transfusions do for the body? Well that is more or less what the Communion of Saints does for the soul.

545 Live a particular Communion of Saints: and each one will feel, at the time of interior struggle, just as at the time of professional work, the joy and the strength of not being alone.

546 Son, how well you lived the Communion of Saints, when you wrote to me: "Yesterday I *felt* that you were praying for me"!

547 Someone else who knows about this

"communication" of supernatural riches, tells me: "The letter did me a lot of good: I could feel everyone's prayers behind it!... and I very much need to be prayed for."

548 If you feel the Communion of Saints, if you live it, you will gladly be a man of penance. –And you will come to realise that penance is *gaudium, etsi laboriosum,* joy, albeit toilsome: and you will feel yourself "allied" to all the penitent souls that have been, that are and that ever will be.

549 You will find it easier to do your duty if you think of the help you are getting from your brothers and of the help you are not giving them, if you are not faithful.

550 *Ideo omnia sustineo propter electos,* I endure all things for the sake of the elect, *ut et ipsi salutem consequantur,* that they too may obtain the salvation, *quae est in Christo Iesu,* that is in Christ Jesus.

–What a good way of living the Communion of Saints!

–Ask Our Lord to give you this spirit of Saint Paul.

DEVOTIONS

551 Let us flee from "routine" as from the devil himself. –The great means to avoid falling into this abyss, the sepulchre of true piety, is constant presence of God.

552 Have few private devotions, but be constant in them.

553 Don't forget your childhood prayers, learned perhaps from your mother's lips. –Say them each day with simplicity, as you did then.

554 Don't omit the Visit to the Blessed Sacrament. –After your usual vocal prayer, tell Jesus, really present in the Tabernacle, about the cares and worries of your day.

–And you will get light and encouragement for your life as a Christian.

555 How truly lovable is the Sacred Humanity of our God! –You "entered" into the most holy Wound of your Lord's right hand, and you asked me: "If one of Christ's Wounds cleanses, heals, soothes, strengthens and kindles and enraptures, what will the five not do, open on the wood?"

556 The Way of the Cross. –Here indeed is a sturdy and fruitful devotion! May you get used to going over those fourteen points of Our Lord's Passion and Death, each Friday. –I assure you that you will draw strength for the whole of the week.

557 Christmas devotion. –I don't smile when I see you putting up cardboard mountains for the Crib and placing simple clay figures around the Manger. –You have never seemed more a man to me than now, when you seem to be a child.

558 The Holy Rosary is a powerful weapon. Use it with confidence and you will be amazed at the results.

559 Saint Joseph, Father of Christ, is also your Father and Lord. –Have recourse to him.

560 Our Father and Lord Saint Joseph is a Master of the interior life. –Place yourself under his patronage and you'll feel the effectiveness of his power.

561 Speaking of Saint Joseph in the book of her life, Saint Teresa says: "If anyone cannot find a Master to teach him how to pray, let him take this glorious Saint as his master and he will not go astray." –This is advice from an experienced soul. Follow it.

562 Confide in your Guardian Angel. –Treat him as a very dear friend, that's what he is, and he will render you a thousand services in the ordinary affairs of each day.

563 Win over the Guardian Angel of that person whom you wish to draw to your apostolate. –He is always a great "accomplice".

564 If you were aware of the presence of your Guardian Angel and those of your neighbours you would avoid many of the foolish things which come out in conversation.

565 You are amazed because your Guardian Angel has done you such obvious favours. –And you should not be amazed: that's why Our Lord has placed him at your side.

566 You say that in such surroundings there are many occasions of going astray? –All right. But, are there not also Guardian Angels?

567 Turn to your Guardian Angel, at the moment of trial, and he will protect you from the devil and bring you holy inspirations.

568 How joyfully the Holy Guardian Angels must have done their duty toward that soul who said to them: "Holy Angels, I call on you, like the Spouse in the Canticle of Canticles, *ut nuntietis ei quia amore* *langueo,* to tell him that I am dying of Love."

569 I know you will be glad to have this prayer to the Holy Guardian Angels of our Tabernacles:

Oh Angelic Spirits who guard our Tabernacles, wherein lies the adorable treasure of the Holy Eucharist, defend it from profanation and preserve it for our love.

570 Drink at the clear fountain of the Acts of the Apostles: In the twelfth chapter Peter, freed from prison by the ministry of Angels, makes his way to the house of Mark's mother. –They refuse to believe the servant-girl, who declares that Peter is at the door. *Angelus eius est!* "It must be his Angel!" they said.

–See on what intimate terms the early Christians were with their Guardian Angels.

– And you?

571 The holy souls in purgatory. –Out of charity, out of justice, and out of an excusable selfishness – they have such power with God! – be very much aware of them in your sacrifices and in your prayer.

May you be able to say, when you speak of them: "My good friends the souls in purgatory..."

572 You ask me why I always recommend you, so earnestly, to use holy water each day. –I could give you many reasons. This one from the Saint of Avila will, I'm sure, be enough for you: "From nothing do the devils flee more, never to return, than from holy water."

573 Thank you, my God, for the love for the Pope which you have placed in my heart.

574 Who told you that to make novenas is not a manly practice? –Such devotions are manly, when a manly person does them..., in a spirit of prayer and penance.

FAITH

575 Some people pass through life as through a tunnel, without ever understanding the splendour and the security and the warmth of the sun of faith.

576 With what infamous lucidity does Satan argue against our Catholic Faith!

But, let us say to him always, without entering into any debate: I am a son of the Church.

577 You feel a gigantic faith... –He who gives you that faith, will give you the means.

578 It is Saint Paul who says it to you, apostolic soul: *Iustus ex fide vivit,* the just

man lives by faith.

How is it that you are letting that fire die out?

579 Faith. –It is sad to see how abundantly many Christians have it on their lips, and how sparingly they put it into their actions.

–It would seem to be a virtue to be preached only, and not to be practised.

580 Humbly ask God to increase your faith. –And then, with new lights, you will be able to judge correctly the differences between the paths of the world and your way as an apostle.

581 How humbly and simply the Gospel writers relate incidents that show up the weak and wavering faith of the Apostles!

–So that you and I won't lose hope of eventually having the strong unshakable faith those first few had afterwards.

582 How beautiful is our Catholic Faith! –It provides a solution for all our anxieties, and calms our mind and fills our heart with hope.

583 I don't go looking for "miracles". –I have told you that I can find more than enough miracles in the Holy Gospel to confirm my faith. –But I can't help pitying those Christians, even pious, "apostolic!" people, who smile when they hear of extraordinary ways, of supernatural events. –I feel a longing to say to them: Yes, there are also miracles taking place today: *we* would work them if we had faith!

584 Stir up the fire of your faith. –Christ is not a figure who has passed. He is not a memory that is lost in history.

He lives!: *Iesus Christus heri et hodie: ipse et in saecula!* says Saint Paul: Jesus Christ yesterday and today and for ever!

585 *Si habueritis fidem, sicut granum sinapis!* –If you had faith as great as a tiny grain of mustard-seed!...

–What promises are contained in this exclamation of the Master!

586 God is Himself always. –Men of faith are needed: and there will be a renewal of the wonders we read of in Sacred Scripture.

–*Ecce non est abbreviata manus Domini,* God's arm, his power, has not grown weaker!

587 They don't have faith. –But they have superstitions. We laughed and felt embarrassed when that influential person became unnerved on hearing a particular word, in itself harmless and inoffensive, but which, for him, was a bad omen, or on seeing a chair being swivelled on one leg.

588 *Omnia possibilia sunt credenti.* "All things are possible for him who believes." –The words are Christ's.

–How is it that you don't say to him with the apostles: *Adauge nobis fidem!* "Increase my faith!"?

HUMILITY

589 When you hear the applause of triumph, let there also sound in your ears the laughter you provoked with your failures.

590 Don't wish to be like the gilded weather-cock on top of a great building: however much it shines and however high it is, it adds nothing to the solidity of the building.

–Rather be like an old stone block hidden in the foundations, under ground, where no one can see you: because of you the house will not fall.

591 The more I am exalted, my Jesus, the more I want you to humble me in my heart, making me realise what I have been and what I will be, if you leave me.

592 Don't forget that you are a... dustbin. –Therefore, if by any chance the divine Gardener lays his hands on you, and scrubs you and cleans you... and fills you with magnificent flowers..., neither the scent nor the colour, that embellish your ugliness, should make you proud.

–Humble yourself: don't you know that you are a rubbish bin?

593 When you come to see yourself as you are, you will think it natural to be despised by others.

594 You're not humble when you humble yourself, but when you are humbled by others and you bear it for Christ.

595 If you knew yourself, you would rejoice in being despised, and your heart would weep at honour and praise.

596 Don't be hurt if people see your faults; the offence against God and the bad

example you may give: that is what should hurt you.

–Apart from this, let them know you as you are and think little of you. –Don't be sorry to be nothing, for then Jesus has to give you everything.

597 If you acted in accordance with the impulses you feel in your heart and with those which reason dictates, you would be constantly flat on the ground, prostrate, like a filthy worm, ugly and despicable... before that God!, who is putting up with so much from you.

598 How great is the value of humility! –*Quia respexit humilitatem*... Over and above faith, charity, immaculate purity, our Mother's joyful hymn in the house of Zachary sings:

"Because he has seen my humility, behold therefore all generations shall call me blessed."

599 You are dust, fallen and dirty. –Even though the breath of the Holy Spirit should lift you above all the things of the earth and make you shine like gold, as your misery reflects in those heights the sovereign rays of the Sun of Justice, do not forget the lowliness of your state.

An instant of pride would cast you back to the ground, and you would cease to be light, becoming mud instead.

600 You?... pride? –About what?

601 Pride? –Why?... Before long – years, days – you will be a heap of rotting flesh: worms, foul-smelling liquids, your shroud in filthy shreds... and no one, on earth, will remember you.

602 You, man of learning, reputation, eloquence, power: if you're not humble, you're worth nothing. –Cut back, uproot that ego of yours, which you've got to such a superlative degree – God will help you – and then you will be able to begin working for Christ, in the lowest place in his army of apostles.

603 That false humility is easy-goingness: that way, apparently humble, you are giving up rights... which are duties.

604 Humbly acknowledge your weakness so that you can say with the Apostle: *Cum enim infirmor, tunc potens sum,* For when I am weak, then I am strong.

605 "Father, how do you put up with all this rubbish?" you asked me, after a contrite confession.

–I said nothing, but thought that if your humility makes you feel like that – rubbish: a heap of rubbish! – we may yet turn all your wretchedness into something really great.

606 See how humble our Jesus is: a... donkey was his throne in Jerusalem!...

607 Humility is another good way to reach interior peace. –*He* has said so: "Learn from me, for I am meek and humble of heart... and you will find peace for your souls."

608 It is not a lack of humility to be aware of the progress of your soul. –That way you can thank God for it.

–But don't forget that you are a poor little fellow, wearing a good suit... on loan.

609 Self-knowledge leads us by the hand, as it were, to humility.

610 Your firmness, in defence of the spirit and norms of the apostolate in which you work, should not weaken through false humility. –That firmness is not pride: it is the cardinal virtue of fortitude.

611 Because of pride. –You were beginning to think that you, by yourself, were equal to anything. –He left you for a moment, and you fell headlong. –Be humble and his extraordinary aid will not be denied you.

612 You may as well get rid of those proud thoughts: you are what the brush is in the hands of the artist. –And nothing more.

–Tell me: of what use is a brush, if it doesn't let the painter do his work?

613 In order to be humble, you, who are so empty and self-satisfied, all you need is to consider these words of Isaiah: you are "A drop of water or dew that falls on the ground and is scarcely seen."

OBEDIENCE

614 In apostolic works there is no such thing as a trifling disobedience.

615 Temper your will, strengthen your will: let it become, with God's grace, like a spur of steel.

–Only by being strong-willed can you know how not to be so in order to obey.

616 With that slowness, with that passivity, with that reluctance of yours to obey, how the apostolate suffers and what satisfaction you give to the enemy!

617 Obey, as an instrument obeys in the hands of the artist – it doesn't stop to consider why it's doing this or that – knowing

for sure that you will never be told to do anything that is not good and for all the glory of God.

618 The enemy: Will you obey... even in this "ridiculous" little detail? –You, with God's grace: I will obey... even in this "heroic" little detail.

619 Initiatives. –You should have them, in your apostolate, within the guidelines of the mandate you have received.

–If they go beyond those limits or if you are in doubt, consult your superior, without telling anyone else what you are thinking.

–Never forget that you are only an executor.

620 If obedience doesn't give you peace, it's because you're proud.

621 What a pity that the person in charge may not be giving you good example!... –But, is it for his personal qualities that you obey him?... Or that *Obedite praepositis vestris* –"Obey your superiors", of Saint

Paul, do you conveniently translate it with an interpolation of your own, which more or less comes to say... "Always provided the superior has virtues to my taste"?

622 How well you've understood obedience when you write to me: "To obey always is to be a martyr without dying"!

623 You have been told to do something you think useless and difficult. –Do it. –And you'll see it's easy and fruitful.

624 Hierarchy. –Each thing in its place. –What would be left of a Velazquez painting if each colour were to go its own way, if each thread of the canvas were to get loose, if each piece of the wooden stretcher were to separate itself from the others?

625 Your obedience is not worthy of the name if you are not determined to pull down your most flourishing personal work, when told to do so by someone in authority.

626 Isn't it true, Lord, that you were

greatly consoled by the "ingenious" response of that childlike adult who, when he felt disconcerted at having to obey in something unpleasant and in itself repulsive, whispered to you: "Jesus, help me to smile!"?

627 Yours should be a silent obedience. That tongue!

628 Right now, when you are finding it hard to obey, remember your Lord, *factus obediens usque ad mortem, mortem autem crucis,* obedient unto death, even death on a cross!

629 Oh, the power of obedience! –The lake of Genesareth had denied its fishes to Peter's nets. A whole night in vain.

–Then, obediently, he lowered his net again into the water and they caught *piscium multitudinem copiosam,* a great quantity of fishes.

–Believe me, the miracle is repeated each day.

POVERTY

630 Don't forget it: he has most who needs least. –Don't create needs for yourself.

631 Detach yourself from the goods of the world. –Love and practise poverty of spirit: be content with what enables you to live a simple and sober life.

–Otherwise, you will never be an apostle.

632 True poverty does not consist in not having, but in being detached: in voluntarily renouncing one's dominion over things.

–That is why there are poor who are really rich. And vice-versa.

633 If you are a man of God, put the same effort into scorning riches as the men of the world put into possessing them.

634 What attachment to the things of the world! –Soon they will slip from your grasp, for the rich cannot take their riches with them to the grave.

635 You do not have the spirit of poverty, if, when you can choose in such a way that your choice passes unnoticed, you do not choose for yourself what is worst.

636 *Divitiae, si affluant, nolite cor apponere.* –If riches increase, do not set your heart upon them. –Try your best to use them generously. And, if necessary, heroically.

–Be poor in spirit.

637 You do not love poverty if you do not love what poverty brings with it.

638 What holy resources poverty has! –Do you remember? You gave him, at a time of financial distress for that apostolic undertaking, down to the last penny at your disposal.

–And he, a Priest of God, said to you: "I too will give you all that I have." You knelt, and heard: "May the blessing of Almighty God, the Father, the Son and the Holy Spirit, come down upon you and remain for ever."

–You are still convinced that you were well repaid.

DISCRETION

639 Remain silent, and you will never regret it: speak, and you often will.

640 How can you dare ask others to keep a secret..., when your very request is proof that you have not been able to keep it yourself?

641 Discretion is not being mysterious, or secretive. –It is, quite simply, naturalness.

642 Discretion is... refinement. –Do you not feel uneasy, uncomfortable inside, when honest, everyday matters to do with your family emerge from the warmth of the home into the indifference or curiosity of the public gaze?

643 Don't be too easily inclined to disclose intimate details of your apostolate:

don't you see that the world is full of selfishness and misunderstanding?

644 Say nothing: don't forget that your ideal is like a newly-lit flame. –A single breath of air could be enough to snuff it out in your heart.

645 The fruitfulness of silence! –All the energy I see you waste, with your failures in discretion, is energy taken from the effectiveness of your work.

–Be discreet.

646 If you were more discreet you would not experience inside that bad aftertaste which makes you suffer after many of your conversations.

647 Don't expect to be "understood". –That misunderstanding is providential: so that your sacrifice may pass unnoticed.

648 If you keep silent you will achieve greater effectiveness in your apostolic undertakings – for so many people it's all talk and no action! – and you will avoid

many dangers of vainglory.

649 Always looking for results that show! –You ask me for photographs, charts, statistics.

–I won't send you what you ask, because (though I respect the opposite opinion) I would then think I had been working with a view to making good on earth... and where I want to make good is in heaven.

650 There are many people, holy people, who do not understand your way. –Don't insist on getting them to understand: you'll only waste your time and give rise to indiscretions.

651 "The only way to be roots and branches is by being sap, spirit, working on the inside."

–Your friend who wrote those words knew that you were nobly ambitious. –And he showed you the way: discretion, sacrifice, "working on the inside"!

652 Discretion, a virtue of the few. –Who slandered woman by saying that discretion is not a woman's virtue?

–How many men, full-grown men, have yet to learn!

653 What an example of discretion is given us by the Mother of God! Not even to Saint Joseph does she communicate the mystery.

–Ask Our Lady for the discretion you lack.

654 Petty spite has sharpened your tongue. Be quiet!

655 In giving you advice I don't think I could ever over-emphasise the importance of discretion.

–If it's not the cutting edge of your combat weapon, I'll tell you it's the hilt.

656 Hold your tongue whenever you feel indignation surging up within you. –And do so, even when you have very good reason to be angry.

–For, in spite of your discretion, in such moments you always say more than you would have wished.

CHEERFULNESS

657 True virtue is not sad or disagreeable, but pleasantly cheerful.

658 If things go well, let us rejoice, blessing God who gives the increase. –And if they go badly? –Let us rejoice, blessing God who allows us to share in his sweet Cross.

659 The cheerfulness you should have is not the kind we might call physiological, that of a healthy animal, but a different, supernatural, one, which comes from the abandonment of everything and the abandonment of yourself into the loving arms of our Father-God.

660 Never lose heart if you are an apostle. –There is no obstacle you cannot overcome.

–Why are you sad?

661 Long faces..., rough manners..., ridiculous appearance..., unfriendly attitude: is that how you hope to encourage others to follow Christ?

662 You're not cheerful? –Think: there is an obstacle between God and me. –You'll nearly always be right.

663 You ask me to suggest a cure for your sadness. –I'll give you a prescription from an expert hand, the apostle Saint James.

–*Tristatur aliquis vestrum?* –Are you sad, my son? –*Oret!* –Pray! –Try it and you'll see.

664 Don't be gloomy. –Look at things from a point of view that is more... "ours" –more Christian.

665 I want you to be happy always, for

cheerfulness is an essential part of your way.

–Pray that the same supernatural joy may be granted to us all.

666 *Laetetur cor quaerentium Dominum.* –Let the hearts of those who seek the Lord be filled with joy.

–There you have light, to help you look into the reasons for your gloominess.

OTHER VIRTUES

667 Acts of Faith, Hope and Love are valves which provide an outlet for the fire of those souls who live the life of God.

668 Do everything disinterestedly, for pure Love, as if there were neither reward nor punishment. –But foster in your heart the glorious hope of heaven.

669 It is good that you serve God as a son, without payment, generously. –But don't worry if at times you think of the reward.

670 Jesus says: "And whoever leaves home or brothers or sisters or father or mother or wife or children or lands, for my name's sake, will receive a hundredfold and possess everlasting life."

–Let me see you find on earth anyone who pays so generously!

671 Jesus... kept silent. –*Iesus autem tacebat.* –Why do you speak, to console yourself or to explain yourself?

Say nothing. –Seek joy in rebuffs: you will always get fewer than you deserve.

–Can you, by any chance, ask: *Quid enim mali feci?* "What evil have I done?"

672 You can be sure that you are a man of God if you suffer injustice gladly and in silence.

673 What a fine reply was given by that venerable old man to his young friend who complained of the unjust treatment he had suffered:

"So you don't like it?" he said, "Then, give up trying to be good!..."

674 Never give your view if you're not asked for it, even if you think your opinion is the best.

675 It's true that he was a sinner. –But don't classify him irrevocably as such. –Have pity in your heart, and don't forget that he may yet become a Saint Augustine, while you never rise above the mediocre.

676 All the things of this world are no more than dust. –Place them in a heap under your feet, and you will be nearer to heaven.

677 Gold, silver, jewels..., dust, heaps of manure.–Pleasures, sensual delights, satisfaction of the appetites..., like an animal, like a mule, like a pig, like a cock, like a bull.

Honours, distinctions, titles..., thin air, swollen pride, lies, nothing at all.

678 Don't set your heart on loves here below. –Such loves are selfish... Those whom you love will recoil from you, in horror and disgust, within hours of God calling you to his presence. –Elsewhere are the loves that endure.

679 Gluttony is an ugly vice. –Don't you

feel a bit amused, and a bit disgusted too, when you see those dignified gentlemen, seated solemnly round a table and, with an air of ritual, stuffing fatty substances into their digestive tubes, as if the whole thing were an "end" in itself?

680 At meals, don't speak about the food: that's vulgar, unworthy of you. –Speak about something noble – the soul or the mind – and you will dignify this duty.

681 The day you leave the table without having done some small mortification you have eaten like a pagan.

682 You generally eat more than you need. –And that fulness, which often brings you a sense of heaviness and physical discomfort, makes you unfit to savour the supernatural goods and benumbs your mind.

What a fine virtue, even for this earth, temperance is!

683 I see you, Christian gentleman – as you say you are – kissing a picture, mumbling a vocal prayer, crying out against those who attack God's Church... and even frequenting the Holy Sacraments.

But I don't see you making a sacrifice, or avoiding certain conversations... of a "worldly" kind (I could, justifiably, have used a different adjective), or being generous towards those beneath you... or even towards that Church of Christ!, or putting up with a failing in your brother, or getting the better of your pride for some common good, or getting out of your tight cloak of selfishness, or doing... so many other things!

I see you... –I don't see you... –And you... claim to be a Christian gentleman? –What a poor notion you have of Christ!

684 Your talent, your pleasant personality, your qualities... are being wasted: you aren't allowed to make proper use of them. –Think upon these words of a spiritual writer: "Incense offered to God is not wasted. –The Lord is more greatly honoured by the overthrowing of your talents than by the vain use of them."

TRIBULATIONS

685 The whirlwind of persecution is good. –What is the loss?... You can't lose something if it's already lost. –When the tree is not torn up by the roots – and there is no wind or hurricane that can uproot the tree of the Church – only the dry branches fall... And, as for them, they are well fallen.

686 I grant you: that person has behaved badly towards you. –But... haven't you behaved worse towards God?

687 Jesus: wherever you have passed no heart has remained indifferent. –You are either loved or hated.

When a man, an apostle, follows you, carrying out his duty, can I be surprised – for he's another Christ! – that he should arouse similar murmurs of aversion or of love?

688 Once again...: They've said this, they've written that...: in favour, against...: with good, and with not so good will...: half-truths and slanders, panegyrics and plaudits...: inane remarks and others that are spot on...

–You're being silly, utterly silly! Why care, when you are making straight for your goal, your head and heart intoxicated with God, about the clamour of the wind or the chirping of the cricket, or the mooing or the grunting or the braying?...

Besides... it's inevitable: don't try to put gates on an open field.

689 Tongues have been wagging and you have suffered rebuffs that hurt you all the more because you were not expecting them.

Your supernatural reaction should be to pardon, and even to beg pardon, and to take advantage of the experience to detach yourself from creatures.

690 When you meet with suffering, contempt... the Cross, your thought should be: what is this compared with what I deserve?

691 Are you suffering a great tribulation? –Are things going against you? Say, very slowly, as if savouring it, this strong and manly prayer:

"May the most just and most lovable Will of God be done, be fulfilled, be praised and eternally exalted above all things. Amen. Amen."

I assure you that you will find peace.

692 You are suffering in this present life... which is a dream... a short dream. –Rejoice: because your Father-God loves you very much and, if you put no obstacles in his way, after this bad dream, he will give you a good awakening.

693 It hurt you not to be thanked for that favour you did. –Answer me these two questions: Are you all that grateful towards Christ Jesus?... Did you actually do that favour in the hope of being thanked for it on earth?

694 I can't think why you're startled. –Christ's enemies have always been pretty unreasonable.

When Lazarus was raised from the dead, they should have admitted defeat and acknowledged the divinity of Jesus. –But, no: "Let's kill him who gives life!" they said.

And nowadays, they're just the same.

695 In times of struggle and opposition, when perhaps "the good" fill your way with obstacles, lift up your apostle's heart: listen to Jesus as he speaks of the grain of mustard-seed and of the leaven. –And say to him: *Edissere nobis parabolam*, explain the parable to me.

And you'll feel the joy of contemplating the victory to come: birds of the air, sheltering under your apostolate, now in its beginnings; and the whole of the meal leavened.

696 If you receive tribulation with a faint heart you lose your joy and your peace, and you run the risk of not deriving spiritual profit from that trial.

697 Public events have placed you in voluntary confinement, worse perhaps, because of its circumstances, than the confinement of a prison. –You have suffered an eclipse of your personality.

You find no scope, surrounded by selfishness, curiosity, misunderstanding and gossip. –All right: so what? Have you forgotten your sovereignly free will and that power you have as a "child"? –The absence of flowers and leaves (external action) does not exclude growth and activity in the roots (interior life).

Work: things will change in due course, and you will yield more fruit than before, and more tasty too.

698 So you've been told off? –Don't get annoyed, as your pride advises you. –Think: How charitably they're treating me! The things they must have left unsaid!

699 Cross, toil, tribulations: they will be with you as long as you live. –That was the path Christ followed, and the disciple is not above his Master.

700 Agreed: there is a lot of pressure from outside and that excuses you, in part. –But there is also complicity within – take a good look – and there I see no excuse.

701 Have you not heard from the Master's own lips the parable of the vine and the branches? –Take consolation: he's making demands on you, because you are a branch that bears fruit... And he's pruning you, *ut fructum plus afferas,* so that you may yield more fruit.

Of course!: it hurts to be cut back, and pruned. But, afterwards, what lushness in your fruits, what maturity in your works!

702 You are worried. –Look: happen what may in your interior life or in the world around you, never forget that the importance of events or of people is very relative. –Calm down: let time pass; and then, looking at persons and happenings from a distance and without passion, you will see things in perspective; you will put each thing in its proper place and at its proper scale.

If you act this way, you will judge

more fairly and spare yourself many a worry.

703 A bad night, in a bad inn. –That, they say, was Saint Teresa of Avila's definition of this earthly life. –An apt comparison, wouldn't you say?

704 A visit to a famous monastery. –That foreign lady felt moved to pity as she considered the poverty of the building: "You lead a very hard life, don't you?" And the monk, quite happily, said only this: "That's what you wanted, religious friar; that's what you wanted, that's how things are."

These words, which I joyfully heard that holy man say, I can only repeat to you with sorrow, when you tell me you're not happy.

705 Should you get upset? –Never: for to do so means losing your peace.

706 Physical exhaustion. –You feel... a wreck. –Rest. Stop that external activity. –Consult your doctor. Obey, and don't worry.

Soon you will be able to take up your

life again and you will see an improvement, if you're faithful, in your apostolic works.

INTERIOR STRUGGLE

707 Don't be troubled if, as you consider the marvels of the supernatural world, you hear that other voice –the intimate, insinuating voice of the old man.

It is "the body of death" crying out for its lost rights... Grace is sufficient for you: be faithful and you will conquer.

708 The world, the devil and the flesh are a band of adventurers who, taking advantage of the weakness of that savage you bear within you, want you to hand over to them, in exchange for the glittering tinsel of a pleasure, which is worth nothing, the pure gold and the pearls and the diamonds and rubies drenched in the living and redeeming blood of your God, which are the price and the treasure of your eternity.

709 Do you hear a voice saying "In a different situation, in another place, at a different level or occupation, you would do much more good. –To do what you're doing no talent is needed!..."?

Well, I say to you: you please God exactly where you've been placed..., and what you have just been thinking is clearly a suggestion of the devil.

710 You get worried and are sad because your Communions are cold and full of dryness. –When you go to the Sacrament, tell me: are you seeking yourself or are you seeking Jesus? –If you are seeking yourself, you have reason to be sad... But if, as you ought, you are seeking Christ, could you ask for a surer sign than the Cross that you have found him?

711 Another fall... and what a fall!... Should you give up hope? No: humble yourself and have recourse, through Mary, your Mother, to the Merciful Love of Jesus. –A *miserere,* "Lord, have mercy", and lift up your heart! –Begin again.

712 How low you have fallen! –Begin the foundations from down there. –Be humble. –*Cor contritum et humiliatum, Deus, non despicies.* –God will not disdain a contrite and humbled heart.

713 You're not going against God. –Your falls are due to weakness. –I'll take your word for it: but... those weaknesses are so frequent! – you seem unable to avoid them – that, if you don't want me to think you bad, I shall have to think you are both bad and stupid.

714 You're wanting to, without really wanting to, as long as you don't put the occasion firmly aside. –Don't try to fool yourself by telling me you're weak. You're a... coward, which is not the same thing.

715 That fear and trepidation in your spirit, the temptation, which envelops you, is like a blindfold over the eyes of your soul.

You are in darkness. –Don't insist on walking alone, for, alone, you will fall. –Go to your Director – to your superior –

and he will bring to your ears those words of Raphael the Archangel to Tobias:

Forti animo esto, in proximo est ut a Deo cureris. "Be of courage, thy cure from God is at hand." –Be obedient, and the scales will fall, the blindfold will fall from your eyes, and God will fill you with grace and with peace.

716 I don't know how to conquer myself!, you write to me despondently. –And I answer: But, have you really tried to use the means?

717 Fortunate misfortunes of this world! –Poverty, tears, hatred, injustice, dishonour... You will be able to do all things in Him who strengthens you.

718 You are suffering... and you would like not to complain. –It doesn't matter if you complain, it's the natural reaction of our poor flesh, as long as your will wants for you, now and always, whatever God wants.

719 Never despair. Dead and decayed was Lazarus: *Iam foetet, quatriduanus est* *enim* –"By this time there will be an odour, for he has been buried four days," Martha says to Jesus.

If you hear God's inspiration and follow it – *Lazare, veni foras!* "Lazarus, come forth!" – you will come back to Life.

720 It's hard! –Yes, I know. But, keep going!: for no one will be rewarded – and what a reward! – but him who fights bravely.

721 If your spiritual edifice is tottering, if everything seems to be up in the air... find your support in a filial confidence in Jesus and Mary, the sure and steady rock on which you should have built from the beginning.

722 It's a long trial this time. –Perhaps, and even without the perhaps, you haven't borne it well so far... because you were still seeking human consolations. –And your Father-God has torn them out by the roots so as to leave you nothing to cling to but Him.

723 So it's all the same to you? –Don't try to fool yourself. Right now, if I were to ask you about certain people and undertakings, in which for God's love you've put your whole soul, you would answer me, eagerly!, with the interest of someone speaking of what is his own.

It isn't all the same to you: it's just that you're not tireless..., and you need more time for yourself: time that will also be for your activities, since, after all, you are the instrument.

724 You tell me that in your breast you have fire and water, cold and heat, fatuous passions and God...: one candle lit to Saint Michael, and another to the devil.

Set your mind at rest: as long as you want to fight there aren't two candles burning in your breast, but only one, the Archangel's.

725 The enemy almost always works that way with souls who are going to resist him: hypocritically, gently: with motives... of a spiritual nature!: not attracting attention... –And then, when there seems to be no remedy (there is), he comes brazenly... trying to bring about a Judas-like despair, with no repentance.

726 After losing those human consolations you are left with a feeling of lonelyness, as if you were hanging by a mere thread over the black emptiness of an abyss. –And your cries, your shouts for help, seem to be heard by nobody.

You really deserve that desolation. –Be humble, don't seek yourself, or seek your own comfort: love the Cross – to bear it is hardly enough – and Our Lord will hear your prayer. –And your senses will calm down. –And your heart will heal again. –And you will have peace.

727 Everything seems to touch you on the raw, to make you suffer in your faculties and in your senses. And everything is a temptation to you...

Be humble, I insist: you will see how quickly all this passes: and the pain will be turned into joy: and the temptation, into firm purpose.

But, in the meantime, strengthen

your faith; fill yourself with hope; and make constant acts of Love, even though you think they are only on your lips.

728 All our fortitude is on loan.

729 Oh, my God: each day I am less sure of myself and more sure of You!

730 If you don't leave Him, He won't leave you.

731 Rely on Jesus for everything: you have nothing, are worth nothing, can do nothing. –He will act, if you abandon yourself in Him.

732 Oh, Jesus! –I rest in Thee.

733 Trust always in your God. –He does not lose battles.

LAST THINGS

734 "This is your hour and the power of darkness," –So, the sinful man has his hour? –Yes... and God his eternity!

735 If you're an apostle, death for you will be a good friend who helps you on your way.

736 Have you seen, on a sad autumn evening, how dead leaves fall? Thus each day do souls fall into eternity: one day, the falling leaf will be you.

737 Have you heard how sadly the worldly-minded lament that "Each day that passes is to die a little"?

Well, I say to you: rejoice, apostolic

soul, because each day that passes brings you closer to Life.

738 For "others", death halts them and startles them. –For us, death – Life – is an encouragement and a stimulus.

For them it is the end: for us, the beginning.

739 Don't be afraid of death. –Accept it, from now on, generously..., when God wills it..., as God wills it..., where God wills it. –Have no doubt: it will come at the time, in the place and in the way that are most fitting..., sent by your Father-God. –Welcome be our sister death!

740 What part of the world will collapse if I am not there, if I die?

741 Have you seen the physical disintegration, giving off foul-smelling odours, of the corpse of a person one loved? –Well, that is the body beautiful!– Contemplate it and draw your own conclusions.

742 Those paintings by Valdés Leal,* with so much distinguished carrion – bishops, knights of the military orders – in a state of living decay, I can't believe they do not move you.

What then do you say of the Duke of Gandía's• cry: "No more will I serve a lord who can die on me"?

743 You talk to me about dying "heroically". –Don't you think it's more "heroic" to die unnoticed, in a good bed, like a bourgeois..., but to die of Love?

744 You –if you are an apostle– will not have to die. –You will move house, that's all.

745 "He shall come to judge the living and the dead," we say in the Creed. –May you never lose sight of that judgement and of that justice and... of that Judge.

746 Does your soul not burn with the

---

* Juan de Valdés Leal (1622-1690): Spanish painter famous for his paintings depicting death.

• Duke of Gandía: later St Francis Borgia (1510-1572).

desire to make your Father-God happy when he has to judge you?

747 There is a great tendency among worldly souls to remind themselves of God's Mercy. –And so they find encouragement to persist in their follies.

It is true that God Our Lord is infinitely merciful, but he is also infinitely just: and there is a judgement, and He is the Judge.

748 Courage. –Don't you know that Saint Paul says, to the Corinthians, that "Each shall receive his own wages, according to his labour"?

749 There is a hell. –A statement which, to you, might sound like a platitude. –I'm going to repeat it for you: there is a hell!

Echo it for me, at the right moment, in the ear of that companion of yours... and of that other one.

750 Listen to me, you who are immersed in science up to your eyebrows: your science cannot deny the reality of diabolic activities. My Mother, the Holy Church – for many years, and it's also a praiseworthy private devotion – required her Priests to invoke Saint Michael each day at the foot of the altar, *contra nequitiam et insidias diaboli*, against the wickedness and snares of the enemy.

751 Heaven: "Eye has not seen, nor ear heard, neither has it entered into the heart of man to conceive the things that God has prepared for those who love him."

Don't these revelations of the Apostle spur you on to fight?

752 Always. –For ever! –Words soiled and cheapened by our human desire to prolong, to eternalise, what is pleasant.

Lying words, on earth, where everything comes to an end.

753 This, life on this earth, is continually passing away: hardly has pleasure begun than it is already ended.

THE WILL OF GOD

754 This is the key to open the door and enter the Kingdom of Heaven: *Qui facit voluntatem Patris mei qui in coelis est, ipse intrabit in regnum coelorum* –"He that does the will of my Father...", he shall enter!

755 On whether you and I behave as God wants, don't forget it, many great things depend.

756 We are stones, blocks of stone, that can move and feel, that have a totally free will.

God himself is the stone-cutter who removes our rough edges, shaping us, modifying us as He desires, with blows of the hammer and chisel.

Don't let us try to draw aside, don't let us want to side-step his Will for, in any case, we won't be able to avoid the blows. –We will suffer all the more and uselessly, and, instead of polished stone ready for the work of building, we will be a shapeless heap of rubble that people will trample contemptuously under foot.

757 Resignation?... Conformity?... *Love* for the Will of God!

758 A wholehearted acceptance of the Will of God necessarily brings joy and peace: happiness in the Cross. –It's then one sees that Christ's yoke is sweet and that his burden is not heavy.

759 Peace! Peace!, you say to me. –Peace is... for men of "good" will.

760 A thought which brings peace to the heart and which the Holy Spirit gives ready-made to those who love God's Will: *Dominus regit me, et nihil mihi deerit* – "The Lord rules over me, there is nothing I shall want."

What can worry a soul who sincerely repeats these words?

761 Free man, subject yourself to voluntary servitude so that Jesus will not have to say of you what we are told he said of others to Saint Teresa: "Teresa, I wanted... But men did not."

762 An act of identification with the Will of God:

"Do you want it, Lord?... Then I want it too!"

763 Don't hesitate: let your lips pronounce a heartfelt *Fiat,* "Be it done!"..., which will be the crowning of your sacrifice.

764 The closer an apostle is to God, the more universal he feels: his heart expands, taking in everybody and everything in its longing to lay the universe at the feet of Jesus.

765 I love your Will so much, my God and want it to be done more than, if such an absurdity could be, getting to heaven without fulfilling it.

766 Abandonment to the Will of God is the secret of happiness on earth. –Say, then: *Meus cibus est, ut faciam voluntatem eius,* My food is to do his Will.

767 That abandonment is precisely what you need in order not to lose your peace from now on.

768 *Gaudium cum pace,* joy and peace, is the sweet and certain fruit of abandonment.

769 Holy indifference is not dryness of heart... just as the heart of Jesus wasn't dry.

770 You're not less happy with too little than with too much.

771 God exalts those who carry out his will in the very thing in which he humbled them.

772 Ask yourself many times a day: Am I doing at this moment what I ought to be doing?

773 Jesus, whatever you may *want*... I love.

774 Stages: Being resigned to the Will of God; Going along with the Will of God; Wanting the Will of God; Loving the Will of God.

775 Lord, if it is your Will, make of my poor flesh a Crucifix.

776 Don't fall into a vicious circle. You are thinking: When this is settled this way or that other way I will be very generous with my God.

Mightn't it be that Jesus is waiting for you to be generous without reserve, so that He can settle things far better than you can imagine?

A firm resolution, as a logical consequence: at each moment of each day I will try to carry out generously the Will of God.

777 Your own will, your own judgement: that's what troubles you.

778 It only takes a few seconds... Just think, before starting anything: What does God want of me in this?

Then, with God's grace, do it!

THE GLORY OF GOD

779 It is good to give glory to God, without seeking foretastes (wife, children, honours...) of that glory, which we will enjoy fully with Him in the Life to come...

Besides, He is generous... He gives a hundredfold: and this is true even in children. –Many give them up for the sake of his glory, and they have thousands of children of their spirit. –Children, as we are children of our Father, who is in heaven.

780 *Deo omnis gloria.* –All glory to God. –This is a categorical confession of our nothingness. He, Jesus, is everything. We, without Him, are worth nothing: nothing.

Our vainglory would be just that: vain glory; it would be a sacrilegious robbery: the "I" should not appear anywhere..

781 Without me, you can do nothing, Our Lord has said. –And he has said it so that you and I would never credit ourselves with successes that are his. –*Sine me, nihil!...*

782 How can you dare use that spark of the divine intelligence – your mind – in anything but in giving glory to your Lord?

783 If life did not have as its purpose to give glory to God, it would be contemptible, even worse: abhorrent.

784 Give "all" the glory to God. –Use your will, aided by grace, to "squeeze out" each of your actions, so that there remains in them nothing that smacks of human pride, of self-complacency.

785 *Deus meus es tu, et confitebor tibi: Deus meus es tu, et exaltabo te.* –Thou art my God, and I shall confess thee: Thou art my God, and I shall exalt thee. –A beautiful programme..., for an apostle of your calibre.

786 May no attachment bind you to earth, other than the divine desire of giving glory to Christ and, through Him and with Him and in Him, to the Father and to the Holy Spirit.

787 Rectify, rectify. –What a poor show if your victory were to be made worthless by your having acted from human motives!

788 Purity of intention. –The suggestions of pride and the impulses of the flesh, you recognise them quickly... and you fight and, with grace, you conquer.

But the motives that inspire you, even in the holiest actions, don't seem clear to you... and you hear a voice, deep down inside, which makes you suspect human reasons..., in such a cunning way, that disquiet filters into your soul and you think that you're not acting as you ought – out of pure Love, solely and exclusively to give God all his glory.

React immediately each time and say: "Lord, for myself I want nothing. –It is all for your glory and for Love."

789 Without a doubt you have purified your intention well, when you have said: From this moment on I renounce all human gratitude and reward.

PROSELYTISM

790 Don't you long to shout to the young people milling about you: Fools!, leave those worldly things that curtail the heart... and very often degrade it..., leave those things and come with us in search of Love?

791 You lack "drive". –That's why you sway so few. –It's as if you weren't very convinced of what you gain by giving up those things of the earth for Christ.

Compare: a hundredfold and life everlasting! – Would you call that a poor "bargain"?

792 *Duc in altum.* –Put out to sea! –Throw aside the pessimism that makes a coward of you. *Et laxate retia vestra in capturam,* and let down your nets for a catch.

Don't you see that you can say, as Peter did: *In nomine tuo, laxabo rete,* Jesus, in your name, I will search for souls?

793 Proselytism. –It's the sure sign of true zeal.

794 To sow. –The sower went out... Scatter your seed, apostolic soul. –The wind of grace will take it elsewhere if the furrow where it falls is not worthy... Sow, and be certain that the seed will take root and bear its fruit.

795 By good example good seed is sown; and charity compels everyone to sow.

796 You have but little love if you are not zealous for the salvation of all souls. –You have but poor love if you don't long to pass on your craziness to other apostles.

797 You know that your way is not clear. –And that it is not so because, by not following Jesus closely, you remain in darkness. –What are you waiting for to make up your mind?

798 Reasons?...What reasons could the poor Ignatius have given to the brilliant Francis Xavier?

799 What amazes you seems reasonable enough to me. –So God has sought you out in the practice of your profession?

That's how he sought the first: Peter, Andrew, John and James, by their nets; Matthew, sitting at his tax-collector's bench...

And, wonder of wonders!, Paul, eagerly striving to put an end to the seed of the Christians.

800 The harvest is great and few the labourers. –*Rogate ergo!* –Pray, therefore, to the Lord of the harvest to send out labourers into his harvest.

Prayer is the most effective means of proselytism.

801 Through the world still echoes that divine cry: "It is fire that I have come to spread over the earth, and what will I but

that it be kindled?" –And you see: it has nearly all died out...

Won't you help to spread the blaze?

802 You'd like to attract to your apostolate that brilliant person, and that other one of great influence, and that one, full of prudence and virtues.

Pray, offer up sacrifices and work on them with your example and word. –They won't come! –Don't lose your peace: it's because they're not needed.

Do you think there were no brilliant, and influential, and prudent, and virtuous contemporaries of Peter, outside the apostolate of the first twelve?

803 I'm told you have a "talent", a "knack", for attracting souls to your way.

Be grateful to God for that gift: of being an instrument for seeking instruments!

804 Help me to cry: Jesus, souls!... Apostolic souls! They are for You, for your glory.

You'll see how in the end he will hear us.

805 Tell me: there, where you are... mightn't there be one... or two, who could understand us well?

806 Tell him... yes, that one, that I need fifty men who will love Jesus above all things.

807 You say of that friend of yours that he frequents the Sacraments, that he is clean-living and a good student. –But that he won't "respond": if you speak to him about sacrifice and apostolate, he grows sad and goes away from you.

Don't let it worry you. –It's not a failure of your zeal: it is, to the letter, the scene narrated by the Evangelist: "If you want to be perfect, go and sell all you have, and give it to the poor" (sacrifice)... "and then come, and follow me" (apostolate).

The young man *abiit tristis* –he went away likewise sadfaced: he was unwilling to respond to grace.

808 "A piece of good news: a new madman... for the asylum." –And all is excitement in the "fisherman's" letter.

May God make your nets really effective!

809 Proselytism. –Who does not hunger to perpetuate his apostolate?

810 That consuming desire you have to win new apostles is a sure sign that you have given yourself entirely.

811 Do you remember? –We were doing our prayer, you and I, as night was falling. From close by came the murmur of water. –And, in the stillness of that Castilian city, we heard as well voices speaking in a hundred different tongues, crying out to us in anguish that they do not yet know Christ.

Unashamedly you kissed your Crucifix, and you asked him to make you an apostle of apostles.

812 I can understand that you love your Country and your people so much and that, in spite of these ties, you await impatiently the moment when you will cross lands and seas – going far away! – because your heart is consumed by the thought of the harvest.

LITTLE THINGS

813 Do everything for Love. –That way there are no little things: everything is big. –Perseverance in little things, for Love, is heroism.

814 A little act, done for Love... is worth so much!

815 Do you really want to be a saint? –Carry out the little duty of each moment: do what you ought and concentrate on what you're doing.

816 You have mistaken the way if you disregard little things.

817 "Great" holiness consists in fulfilling the "little duties" of each moment.

818 Great souls pay much attention to little things.

819 Because you have been *in pauca fidelis,* faithful in what is little, enter into the joy of your Lord. –The words are Christ's. *–In pauca fidelis!...* –Now will you disdain little things if heaven itself is promised to those who take care of them?

820 Don't judge by the smallness of the beginnings: it was pointed out to me once that there is no difference in size between seeds that will give annual plants and those that will grow into ageless trees.

821 Don't forget that on earth everything that is great has had a small beginning. –What is born big is monstrous and dies.

822 You tell me: when the opportunity arises to do something big... then! –Then? Are you trying to convince me, and to convince yourself, that you will be able to conquer in the supernatural Olympics, without daily preparation, without training?

823 Did you see how that imposing building was raised? –One brick, and another. Thousands. But, one by one. –And bags of cement, one by one. And blocks of stone, each of them tiny compared with the massive whole. –And bits of iron. –And men working, the same hours, day after day...

Did you see how that imposing building was raised?... –By dint of little things!

824 Haven't you noticed how it's in "tiny" things that human love is shown? –Well, it's also in "tiny" things that divine Love is shown.

825 Keep up with the exact fulfilment of your present obligations. –That work – humble, monotonous, small – is prayer expressed in deeds which dispose you to receive grace for that other work – great and broad and deep – of which you dream.

826 Everything in which we poor human beings intervene – even sanctity – is a tissue of small trifles, which – depending

on the purity of our intention – can form a tapestry of splendid heroism or of meanness, of virtues or of sins.

The epics always tell of gigantic adventures, mingled nevertheless with homely details about the hero. –May you always attach great importance – straightforwardly! – to little things.

827 Have you ever stopped to consider the enormous sum that "many little amounts" can come to?

828 You have had a hard experience: don't forget the lesson. –Your big cowardices now are – it's clear to see – parallel to your little cowardices of each day.

"You haven't been able" to conquer in the big thing, "because you didn't want" to conquer in the little ones.

829 Didn't you see Jesus' eyes light up when the poor widow left her little alms in the temple? –You, give him what you can: the merit doesn't lie in whether it is little or much, but in the good will with which you give it.

830 Please, don't be... silly: it's true that the part you play is, at most, that of a little screw in that great undertaking of Christ's.

But, do you know what happens when a screw is not tight enough or jumps out of place?: bigger parts will also work loose or gear-wheels get damaged or dented.

The work will have been obstructed. –Perhaps the entire machine may be rendered useless.

What a big thing it is to be a little screw!

TACTICS

831 You are, among those around you, apostolic soul, a stone fallen into a lake. –Produce, by your example and your word, a first circle... and this, another... and another, and another... Wider each time.

Now do you understand the greatness of your mission?

832 How anxious people are to get out of place! –What would happen if each bone, each muscle of the human body wanted to occupy a position other than its own?

There is no other reason for the world's discontent. –Persevere in your place, my son: from there... what great work you can do for the effectiveness of Our Lord's kingship!

833 Leaders!... Strengthen your will so that God can make a leader of you. Don't you see how those infamous secret societies work? They've never won over the masses. –In their dens they form a number of demon-men who set to work stirring up the multitudes, driving them mad, so that they will go after them, to the precipice of all excess... and to hell. –They spread an accursed seed.

If you wish..., you will spread the word of God, which is blessed a thousand, thousand times and cannot fail. If you are generous..., if you respond, with your own sanctification, you will obtain that of others: the kingship of Christ: that *Omnes cum Petro ad Iesum per Mariam,* that "All (may go) with Peter to Jesus through Mary".

834 Is there any greater folly than to scatter the golden wheat on the ground to let it rot? –Without that generous folly there would be no harvest.

Son, how are we getting on in generosity?

835 To shine like a star... aspiring to be on high, a light sparkling in the heavens?

Better: to burn, like a torch, hidden, setting your fire to all that you touch. –This is your apostolate: it's for this that you are on earth.

836 To serve as a loud-speaker for the enemy is the height of idiocy; and, if the enemy is an enemy of God, it is a great sin. –That is why, in the professional field, I will never praise the learning of someone who uses that learning as a platform to attack the Church.

837 Galloping, galloping!... Doing things, getting things done!... Feverish, mad urges to be up and doing... Marvellous material constructions...

Spiritually: strips of wood, cheap fabrics, painted cardboard... galloping!, getting things done! –And many people running: coming and going.

The fact is they're working with their eyes on the present moment: they "are" always "in the present". –You... must see things with the eyes of eternity, "keeping present" the final outcome and what has passed...

Calmness. –Peace. –An intense life inside you. Without galloping, without the madness of changing place, from the place that life has assigned to you, like a powerful generator of spiritual electricity, you will give light and energy to so many!..., without losing your own vigour and light.

838 Don't have enemies. –Have only friends: friends... on the right – if they have done or wished to do you good – and... on the left – if they have harmed or attempted to harm you.

839 Don't go into details of "your" apostolate unless it is for the benefit of your neighbour.

840 May your dedication pass unnoticed as that of Jesus did for thirty years.

841 Joseph of Arimathea and Nicodemus visit Jesus hiddenly when things are normal and at the hour of triumph.

But they are courageous, declaring before the authorities their love for Christ *audacter*, boldly, at the hour of cowardice. –Learn.

842 Don't worry if by your deeds "you are known". –It is the good odour of Christ. –Besides, in working always exclusively for Him, you should rejoice to see those words of Scripture being fulfilled: "May they see your good works and glorify your Father who is in heaven."

843 *Non manifeste, sed quasi in occulto* – not with publicity, but hiddenly: thus Jesus goes to the feast of Tabernacles.

Thus will he go, on the way to Emmaus, with Cleophas and his companion. –Thus is he seen, once risen, by Mary of Magdala.

And thus – *non tamen cognoverunt disciupli quia Jesus est*: the disciples did not know that it was He –thus did he appear at the miraculous draught of fishes, as Saint John tells us.

And more hidden still, for Love of men, is he in the Host.

844 Raise magnificent buildings?... Build sumptuous palaces?... Let others raise them... Let others build them...

Souls! –Let us give life to souls... for those buildings... and for those palaces!

What fine houses are being prepared for us!

845 How you made me laugh and how you made me think with that platitude of yours!: "I... always bang nails in point first."

846 Agreed: you do better work with that friendly conversation or that single heart-to-heart chat than by making a great speech – spectacle! spectacle! – in public before thousands of people.

Nevertheless, when speeches have to be made, make them.

847 The efforts of each one of you, taken in isolation, prove ineffective. –If you're united by the charity of Christ, you'll be amazed at their effectiveness.

848 You want to be a martyr. –I'll place a

martyrdom within your reach: to be an apostle and not call yourself an apostle, to be a missionary, with a mission, and not call yourself a missionary, to be a man of God and seem a man of the world: to pass unnoticed!

849 Come on! Laugh at him! –Tell him he's behind the times: it seems incredible that there should still be people who go on believing that the stagecoach is a good means of transport... –That's for those who bring up musty and periwigged "Voltairianisms", or discredited liberalisms of the nineteenth century.

850 What conversations! What vulgarity and how... disgusting! –And you have to live with those people, at the office, at university, in the operating-theatre..., in the world.

If you ask them if they wouldn't mind stopping, they laugh at you. –Look annoyed, and they get worse. –Go away, and they continue.

Here is the solution: first, pray to God for them and make atonement; then...

face them like a man and make use of the "strong language apostolate". –When I next see you I'll whisper in your ear a few useful expressions.

851 Let us channel the "providential imprudences" of youth.

SPIRITUAL CHILDHOOD

852 Try to get to know the "way of spiritual childhood", without *forcing* yourself to follow this path. –Let the Holy Spirit do his work.

853 The way of childhood. –Abandonment. –Spiritual infancy. –All this is not silly nonsense, but a sturdy and solid Christian life.

854 In the spiritual life of childhood the things "children" say or do are never puerile or childish.

855 Spiritual childhood is not spiritual silliness or "soppiness": it is a sane and tough way which, because of its difficult easiness, the soul must begin and continue led by the hand of God.

856 Spiritual childhood requires submission of the mind, which is harder than submission of the will. –In order to subject the mind we need, as well as God's grace, a continual exercise of the will, which says "No", just as it says "No" to the flesh, again and again and always; and so we have the paradox that whoever follows the "Little way of childhood", in order to become a child, needs to add strength and manliness to his will.

857 To be little: the great feats of daring are always those of children. –Who cries for... the moon? –Who pays no heed to danger to get what he wants?

"Place" in "such" a child, much grace from God, the desire to do his Will (God's), great love for Jesus, all the human knowledge he is capable of acquiring... and you will have a portrait of the character of the apostles of today, such as God undoubtedly wants them.

858 Be a child. –Even more so. –But don't stop at the "show-off age": have you ever seen anything sillier than a little child pretending to be a "big fellow", or a grown man acting like a "baby"?

A child, with God: and, just because of that, very much a man in everything else. –Ah!: and drop those lap-dog manners.

859 At times we feel inclined to do childish things. –They're little deeds with a wonderful value in God's eyes and, as long as we don't let routine creep in, such deeds will indeed be fruitful, just as Love is always fruitful.

860 Before God, who is eternal, you are a smaller child than, before you, a two-year old toddler.

And, as well as being a child, you are a son of God. –Don't forget it.

861 Child, enkindle in your heart an ardent desire to atone for the enormities of your life as an adult.

862 Silly child: the day you hide something to do with your soul from your Director, you have ceased to be a child, for you will have lost your simplicity.

863 Child, when you really are one, you will be all-powerful.

864 Being children you will have no worries: children quickly forget what's troubled them and return to their usual games. –And so, with abandonment, you will not have to worry, for you will rest in the Father.

865 Child, offer him each day... even your frailties.

866 Good child: offer him the work of those labourers who do not know him; offer him the natural good spirits of those poor little ones who go to godless schools...

867 Children have nothing of their own, everything belongs to their parents... and your Father always knows best how to manage the family patrimony.

868 Be small, very small. –No older than two years old, three at most. –For older children are little rascals who already are trying to deceive their parents with improbable lies.

It is because they have the wickedness, the *fomes* or inclination to sin, but they lack the experience of evil, which will teach them the science of sinning, so that they can cover up the falseness of their deceits with an appearance of truth.

They have lost their simplicity, and simplicity is indispensable to be children before God.

869 But, child!: why do you keep trying to walk on stilts?

870 Don't wish to be grown-up. –A child, always a child, even if you are dying of old age. –When a child stumbles and falls, nobody is surprised...: his father promptly lifts him up.

When the person who stumbles and falls is a grown-up, the first reaction is to laugh. –Sometimes, after that first impulse, the sense of ridicule gives way to pity. –But grown-ups have to get up by themselves.

Your sad experience each day is full of stumbles and falls. What would become of you if you were not continually more of a child?

Don't wish to be grown-up. –A child, so that, when you stumble, you will be lifted up by the hand of your Father-God.

871 Child, abandonment requires docility.

872 Don't forget that Our Lord has a predilection for little children and for those who become as little children.

873 Paradoxes of a little soul. –When Jesus sends you things which the world calls good, weep in your heart at the thought of His goodness and your malice; when Jesus sends you things which people consider bad, be glad in your heart, for He always gives you what is fitting and then it's the beautiful moment of loving the Cross.

874 Daring child, cry out: What love Teresa had! –What zeal Francis Xavier had! –What a wonderful man Saint Paul was! –Ah, Jesus, well I... I love you more than Paul, Francis Xavier and Teresa!

LIFE OF CHILDHOOD

875 Don't forget, silly child, that Love has made you all-powerful.

876 Child: don't lose your loving habit of "storming" Tabernacles.

877 When I call you a 'good child' don't think I imagine you shy or bashful. –If you are not manly and... normal, instead of being an apostle you will be a caricature and a laughing stock.

878 Good child: say to Jesus many times a day: I love you, I love you, I love you...

879 When you are troubled by your wretchedness don't let yourself get sad.

–Glory in your infirmities, like Saint Paul, for children are permitted, without fear of ridicule, to imitate the great.

880 Let not your faults and imperfections, or even your serious falls, separate you from God. –A weak child, if he is wise, tries to keep close to his father.

881 Don't worry, if you get annoyed, when you are doing those little things He asks of you. –The time will come when you will smile...

Have you ever seen how reluctantly a little child gives his father, who is testing him, the sweet he had in his hands? –But, he gives it to him: love has conquered.

882 When you want to do things well, really well, it turns out that you do them worse. –Humble yourself before Jesus and say to him: Don't you see how badly I do everything? –Well, if you don't help me a lot, I'll do it even worse!

Have pity on your child: you see, I want to write a big page each day in the book of my life... But, I'm so clumsy!, that if the Master doesn't guide my hand, instead of graceful strokes, my pen leaves behind blots and scrawls that can't be shown to anyone.

From now on, Jesus, we'll always do the writing together.

883 I admit that my clumsiness, my Love, is so great... so very great, that even when I wish to caress I cause pain. –Make the manners of my soul more gentle: give me, I'd like you to give me, within the sturdy manliness of the life of childhood, the gentleness and affection that children have when they express their intimate outpourings of Love towards their parents.

884 You are full of miserable failings. –Each day you see them more clearly. –But don't let them frighten you. –He well knows that you can't yield more fruit.

Your involuntary falls, a child's falls, mean that your Father-God will take greater care and your Mother Mary will not let you go from her loving hand: make the most of it and, when each day Our Lord picks you up from the ground, embrace him with all your strength and lay your wretched head upon his open breast, so as to be driven to utter distraction by the beating of his most lovable Heart.

885 One pinprick. –And another. And another. –Suffer them! Don't you see that you are so small that the only thing you can offer in your life, in your little way, are those little crosses?

Besides, just think: one cross upon another – one pinprick..., and another..., what a huge pile!

Finally, child, you will have learned to do a really big thing: to Love.

886 When a childlike soul makes Our Lord know of its desires to be forgiven, it can be sure that it will soon see those desires fulfilled: Jesus will tear away from that soul the filthy tail that it drags behind it on account of its past miseries; he will remove the dead-weight, remaining after all those impurities, which glues it to the ground; he will cast far away from the child all the earthly ballast in its heart so that it can rise up towards God's Majesty, there to melt in the living flame of Love, which is God Himself.

887 That discouragement brought on by your failures in generosity, your falls, your relapses – only apparent perhaps – often makes you feel that you have broken something of exceptional value (your sanctification).

Don't be worried: apply to your supernatural life the wise way simple children have for solving such a conflict.

They have broken – through frailty, nearly always – something their father values greatly. –They are sorry, perhaps they shed tears, but... they go for consolation over their worry to the owner of what has been damaged through their clumsiness..., and their father forgets the value – great though it may be – of the broken object and, full of tenderness, not only forgives, but consoles and reassures the little one. –Learn.

888 Let your prayer be manly. –Being a child does not mean being effeminate.

889 For one who loves Jesus, prayer,

even prayer with dryness, is the sweetness that always puts an end to sorrow: one goes to prayer with the eagerness of a child going for sugar, after taking a bitter dose of medicine.

890 You get distracted in prayer. –Try to avoid distractions, but don't worry if, in spite of everything, you're still distracted.

Don't you see how, in ordinary life, even the most sensible children amuse themselves and play about with the things around them, and often don't pay attention to what their father is saying? –This does not imply any lack of love, or respect: it is just the feebleness and littleness proper to a child.

Well, look: you are a child before God.

891 When you pray keep untimely ideas moving, just as if you were a warden on traffic duty: that's why you have the energetic will-power your life of childhood has given you. –Now and then, halt some such thought for a while, to pray for those who figured in that untimely memory.

Then, off again!... And so on, until the time is up. –When your prayer has been this way and you think it's useless, rejoice and believe that you have succeeded in pleasing Jesus.

892 What a wonderful thing it is to be a child! –When a man asks a favour, his request must be backed by a list of his qualifications.

When it is a child who asks – since children haven't any qualifications – it's enough to say: I'm a son of So-and-so.

Ah, Lord! – say to him, with all your heart! – I am... a son of God!

893 Perseverance. –A child knocking at a door knocks once, twice, many times... loud and long, shamelessly! And the anger of whoever comes to open is disarmed by the simplicity of the annoying little creature... –So you with God.

894 Have you witnessed the gratitude of little children? –Imitate them, saying, as they do, to Jesus, when things are favourable and when they aren't: "How good you are! How good!..."

These words, truly meant, are the way of childhood, which will lead you to peace, with balance and measure in laughter and tears, but without balance and measure in Love.

895 Your work has exhausted you, and you are unable to pray. You are always in the presence of your Father. –If you can't speak to him, look at him every now and then like a little child does... and He will smile at you.

896 You say that in your thanksgiving after Communion the first thing that comes to your lips, without your being able to help it, is petition...: Jesus, give me this; Jesus, that soul; Jesus, that undertaking?

Don't worry or try to force yourself: haven't you seen how, when there is a loving father and a simple and daring child, the little lad puts his hand into his father's pocket, looking for sweets, before greeting him with a kiss? –Well then...

897 Our will, strengthened by grace, is

all-powerful before God. –Thus, at the sight of so many offences against Our Lord, if we say to Jesus and really mean it, as we travel on a tram for example: "My God, I'd like to make as many acts of love and reparation as turns of the wheel of this vehicle", at that very instant, in the eyes of Jesus, we really have loved him and atoned just as we desired.

Such "nonsense" is not pushing spiritual childhood too far: it is the eternal dialogue between the innocent child and his father doting on his son:

–"How much do you love me? Tell me!" –And the little lad pipes up: "Ma-ny, ma-ny mil-lion!"

898 If you live the "life of childhood", then, since you are a child, you should be spiritually "greedy". –Call to mind, like children of "your age" do, the treats your Mother keeps in store for you.

And do so many times a day. –It just takes seconds... Mary... Jesus... the Tabernacle... Communion... Love... suffering... the holy souls in purgatory... those who are fighting: the Pope, priests... the faithful...

your own soul... the souls of your people... the Guardian Angels... sinners...

899 That little mortification costs you so much! –You struggle. –It's as if someone were saying to you: Why must you be so faithful to your plan of life, to the clock? –Listen: have you noticed how easily little children are taken in? –They don't want to take some bitter medicine, but... "Come on!" they are told, "This wee spoonful for Daddy, and this one for Granny"... And so on, until they have swallowed the lot.

Why not do the same?: fifteen minutes more cilice for the souls in purgatory; five more for your parents; another five for your brothers in the apostolate... Until you have fulfilled the time allotted in your timetable.

Your mortification done in this way... is worth so much!

900 You are not alone. –Suffer tribulation cheerfully. –It's true, poor child, that you don't feel your Mother's hand in yours. –But... have you never seen mothers in this world, with arms outstretched, following their little ones, when they venture forth, trembling, to take their first steps without help from anyone? –You are not alone: Mary is beside you.

901 Jesus: I can never repay you, even were I to die of Love, for the grace you have showered on me to make me little.

CALLING

902 Why don't you give yourself to God once and for all... really... now!?

903 If you see your way clearly, follow it. –Why don't you shake off the cowardice that holds you back?

904 "Go, preach the Gospel... I will be with you..." –Jesus has said this... and he has said it to you.

905 Patriotic fervour, a praiseworthy thing, leads many men to live a life of "service", of "soldiery". –Please don't forget that Christ too has his "soldiery" and chosen men in his "service".

906 *Et regni eius non erit finis.* –His Kingdom will have no end!

Doesn't it make you glad to work for such a kingdom?

907 *Nesciebatis quia in his quae Patris mei sunt oportet me esse?* –Did you not know that I must be about my Father's business?

A reply from the young Jesus. And a reply made to a mother like his Mother, who had been searching for him for three days, thinking he was lost. –A reply which has as a complement those words of Christ, recorded by Saint Matthew: "Anyone who loves his father or mother more than me, is not worthy of me."

908 You are being too naive when you judge the value of apostolic undertakings by what you can see of them. –With that standard you would have to prefer a hundred-weight of coal to a handful of diamonds.

909 Now that you have given yourself to him, ask him for a new life, a "seal": to confirm the genuineness of your mission as a man of God.

910 That – your ideal, your vocation – is... madness. –And the others – your friends, your brothers – are crazy...

Have you never heard that cry deep down inside you? –Answer, firmly, that you thank God for the honour of being one of those "lunatics".

911 You write to me: "The great longing we all have to see 'this' going ahead and spreading looks as though it's going to turn into impatience. When will we have the explosion, when will the break-through come... when will we see the world ours?"

And you add: "It won't be a useless longing if we pour it into 'coercing' and pleading with God: that way we will have made excellent use of our time."

912 I can understand how you suffer when, in the midst of your enforced inactivity, you consider the work still do be done. –Your heart is too big for this planet, yet it has to adapt itself... to an insignificant routine job.

But tell me, for when are we saving our *fiat* – "be it done"?...

913 Have no doubt about it: your vocation is the greatest grace Our Lord could have given you. –Thank him for it.

914 How pitiful are those crowds – at all social levels, upper, lower and middle – who live without ideals! –They give the impression of not realising that they have souls: they are... a drove, a flock... a herd.

Jesus: we, with the help of your Merciful Love, will turn the drove into a band of followers, the flock into an army..., and from the herd we will draw out, purified, those who no longer wish to be unclean.

915 God's works are not a lever, or a stepping-stone.

916 Lord, make us crazy, with that infectious craziness that will draw many to your apostolate.

917 *Nonne cor nostrum ardens erat in nobis, dum loqueretur in via?* –Was not our heart burning within us, while he spoke to us on the way?

These words of the disciples at Emmaus should rise spontaneously, if you are an apostle, from the lips of your colleagues at work, after meeting you along the ways of their lives.

918 Go to the apostolate to give everything, and not to seek any earthly reward.

919 By wanting you to be an apostle, Our Lord has reminded you, so that you will never forget it, that you are a "son of God".

920 Each one of you must seek to be an apostle of apostles.

921 You are salt, apostolic soul. –*Bonum est sal*, salt is good, we read in the Gospel; *si autem sal evanuerit*, but if salt loses its strength..., it is good for nothing, neither for the soil, nor for manure; it is thrown away as useless.

You are salt, apostolic soul. –But, if you lose your strength...

922 My son: if you love your apostolate, be certain that you love God.

923 The day that you really "get the feel" of your apostolate, that apostolate will serve you as a shield which will blunt all the attacks of your enemies on this earth and from hell.

924 Pray always for perseverance for yourself and for your companions in the apostolate, because our adversary, the devil, knows only too well that you are his great enemies... and if he sees a fall in your ranks, how pleased he is!

925 Just as observant religious are eager to know how the first of their order or congregation lived, so as to adapt themselves to their example, you too – Christian gentleman – should seek to know and imitate the lives of the disciples of Jesus, who knew Peter and Paul and John, and all but witnessed the Death and Resurrection of the Master.

926 You asked me..., and this is my reply: your perfection consists in living perfectly in the place, occupation and position where God, through those in authority, has put you.

927 Pray for one another. –One is wavering?... –And another?...

Keep on praying, without losing your peace. –Some are leaving? Some are being lost?... Our Lord has you numbered from all eternity!

928 You are right. –"Looking down from the peak" you told me "for miles and miles around, there is not a single plain to be seen: behind every mountain, another appears. At times the landscape seems to level out, but then the mist rises and reveals another range that had been hidden."

So it is, so it must be with the horizon of your apostolate: the world has to be crossed. But there are no ways made for you... You yourselves will make them, across the mountains, with the impact of your footprints.

THE APOSTLE

929 The Cross on your breast?... –Fine. But... the Cross on your shoulders, the Cross in your flesh, the Cross in your mind. –That way you will be living through Christ, with Christ and in Christ: only that way will you be an apostle.

930 Apostolic soul: first, yourself. –Our Lord has said, through Saint Matthew: "Many will say to me on the day of judgement: Lord! Lord! Did we not prophesy in your name and cast out devils in your name and work many miracles in your name? Then I will declare to them: I never knew you as mine; depart from me, you workers of iniquity."

God forbid, says Saint Paul, that I,

who have preached to others, should myself be rejected.

931 The military mind of Saint Ignatius has left us a picture of the devil calling up innumerable demons and deploying them through nations, provinces, towns and villages, after a "sermon" in which he charges them to fasten their chains and fetters on the world, leaving not a single person unbound...

You told me you wanted to be a leader: but... what good is a leader in chains?

932 Look: the apostles, for all their evident and undeniable defects, were sincere, simple..., transparent.

You too have evident and undeniable defects. May you not lack simplicity.

933 There is a story of a soul who, on saying to Our Lord in prayer, "Jesus, I love you", heard this reply from heaven: "Love means deeds, not sweet words."

Think about it; mightn't you too deserve this gentle reproach?

934 Zeal is a divine craziness in an apostle which I would like you to have, and it has these symptoms: hunger to know the Master; constant concern for souls; perseverance, that nothing can shake.

935 Don't rest on your laurels. –If, humanly speaking, that attitude is uncomfortable and ill-becoming, what will it be when, as now, the laurels are not yours, but God's?

936 In the apostolate you go to submit yourself, to annihilate yourself: not to impose your own personal viewpoints.

937 Never be men or women of long action and short prayer.

938 Try to live in such a way that you can deprive yourself voluntarily, of the comfort and well-being you wouldn't like to see in the life of another man of God.

Remember you are the grain of wheat the Gospel speaks of. –If you don't bury yourself and die, there will be no harvest.

939 Be men and women of the world, but

don't be worldly men and women.

940 Don't forget that unity is a sign of life: to become disunited is putrefaction, a clear sign of being a corpse.

941 Obedience... a sure way. –Blind obedience to your superior... a way to holiness. –Obedience in your apostolate... the only way: for, in a work of God, the spirit has to be to obey or get out.

942 Bear in mind, my son, that you are not just a soul who has joined other souls to do a good thing.

That's a lot... but it's still little. –You are the Apostle who is carrying out an imperative command from Christ.

943 Be careful that contact with you doesn't make people want to scream like a certain person who exclaimed (and not without reason): "I've had my fill of *decent* people!"

944 You have to pass on your Love of God and zeal for souls to others, so that they in turn may set on fire many more who are on a third plane, and each of these in turn spread the flame to their companions at work.

What a lot of spiritual calories you need! –And what a heavy responsibility if you let yourself grow cold! And, I don't even want to think of it, what a terrible crime if you were to give bad example!

945 It shows a bad disposition if you listen to God's word with a critical spirit.

946 If you want to give yourselves to God in the world, more important than being learned (women don't need to be learned: it's enough if they are discreet),* you must be spiritual, closely united to Our Lord through prayer: you must wear an invisible cloak that will cover each and every one of your senses and faculties: praying, praying and praying; atoning, atoning and atoning.

---

* In Spain, when this book was written, women with degrees were the exception, although the author, even then, encouraged those who spoke to him to follow a university career if this is what they were attracted to. – Trans.

947 You were amazed to hear me approve of the lack of "uniformity" in that apostolate in which you work. And I told you:

Unity and variety. –You should be as different from one another, as are the saints in heaven, for each one has his own very special personal characteristics. –But, also, as alike to one another as are the saints, who would not be saints if each of them had not become identified with Christ.

948 You, beloved child of God, should feel and live our fraternal spirit, but without familiarities.

949 To aspire to positions of leadership in apostolic undertakings is a useless thing in this life, and for the other Life a dangerous one.

If God wants it, you will in time be called. –And then you ought to accept. –But don't forget that wherever you are you can and must become a saint, for that is why you are there.

950 If, when working for Christ, you think that positions of responsibility are anything but a burden, how many bitter disappointments await you!

951 To be in charge of an apostolic undertaking is tantamount to being ready to suffer everything, from everybody, with infinite charity.

952 In apostolic work there can be no excuse for disobedience, or duplicity. –Bear in mind that simplicity is not imprudence, nor indiscretion.

953 You are under an obligation to pray and sacrifice yourself for the person and intentions of whoever is "in charge" of your apostolic undertaking. –If you are remiss in fulfilling this duty, you make me think that you lack enthusiasm for your way.

954 Be particularly respectful towards your superior should he consult you and you have to contradict his opinions. –And never contradict him in the presence of those who are subject to him, even though he may be wrong.

955 In your apostolic undertaking don't fear the enemies outside, however great their power. –This is the real enemy you have to contend with: your lack of "filiation" and your lack of "fraternity".

956 I well understand your being amused by the slights you receive – even though they come from influential enemies – as long as you can feel united to God and to your brothers in the apostolate. –Slighted? Who cares!

957 I frequently compare apostolic work to an engine: gears, pistons, valves, screws...

Well charity – your charity – is the lubricant.

958 Get rid of that "self-satisfied air" which isolates from your soul the souls of those who approach you. –Listen to them. And speak with simplicity: only thus will your work as an apostle grow in extent and fruitfulness.

959 Contempt and persecution are blessed signs of divine predilection, but there is no proof and sign of predilection more beautiful than this: to pass unnoticed.

THE APOSTOLATE

960 Just as the clamour of the ocean is made up of the sound of each of its waves, so the sanctity of your apostolate is made up of the personal virtues of each one of you.

961 You have got to be a "man of God", a man of interior life, a man of prayer and sacrifice. –Your apostolate must be an overflow of your life "within".

962 Unity. –Unity and subjection. What good to me are the loose parts of a clock, even though they are finely wrought, if they cannot tell me the time?

963 I want to see no "cliques" within your work. –That would stunt your apostolates: for if the "clique" managed, at last!, to get control of a universal undertaking... how quickly that universal undertaking itself would become a clique!

964 "There are so many ways!" you told me dejectedly. –There need to be: so that every soul can find its own, within that wonderful variety.

Bewildered? –Choose once and for all: and your bewilderment will change into certainty.

965 Be glad, if you see others working in good apostolic activities. –And pray for them to be given abundant grace of God and to respond to that grace.

Then, you, follow your way: convince yourself you have no other.

966 You show bad spirit if it upsets you to see others working for Christ without regard for what you are doing. –Remember that passage in Saint Mark: "Master, we saw a man casting out devils in your name, though he does not follow us, and we forbade him. Do not forbid him, Jesus replied, for no one who does miracles in my name can then speak ill of me. For he that is not against you, is for you."

967 It's useless to busy yourself in so many external works if you lack Love. –It's like sewing with a needle and no thread.

What a pity, if in the end you had carried out *your* apostolate and not *his* Apostolate!

968 Joyfully I bless you, my son, for that faith in your mission as an apostle, which inspired you to write: "There's no doubt about it: the future is certain, perhaps in spite of us. But it is necessary that we be one with the Head –*ut omnes unum sint!* 'that all may be one!'– through prayer and through sacrifice."

969 Those who, leaving action to others, pray and suffer, will not shine here below, but what a radiant crown will be theirs in the Kingdom of Life! –Blessed be the "apostolate of suffering"!

970 It is true that I have called your discreet apostolate a “silent and effective mission”. –And I don’t take back what I’ve said.

971 I think so highly of your devotion to the early Christians that I will do all I can to encourage it, so that you – like them – will practise, each day with greater enthusiasm, that effective apostolate of discretion and confidence.

972 When you carry out your “apostolate of discretion and confidence”, don’t tell me you don’t know what to say. –For, I will tell you with the psalmist, *Dominus dabit verbum evangelizantibus virtute multa* – The Lord places on his apostles’ lips words filled with efficacy.

973 Those words, whispered in such a timely way in the ear of a friend who is wavering; the helpful conversation, which you managed to start at the right moment; and the professional advice, which improves his university work; and the discreet indiscretion by which you suggest unsuspected horizons for his zeal... This all forms part of the “apostolate of confidence”.

974 “The meal-time apostolate”: it is the old hospitality of the Patriarchs, together with the fraternal warmth of Bethany. –When we practise it, we seem to glimpse Jesus there, presiding, as in the house of Lazarus.

975 There is a pressing need to re-Christianise popular celebrations and customs. –There is a pressing need to avoid public amusements being faced with the dilemma of being either “soppy” or pagan.

Ask Our Lord to provide labourers for this much-needed work, which could be called the “entertainment apostolate”.

976 You praised the “letter apostolate” very effectively when you wrote: “I just can’t manage to fill the page with things likely to help the friend I’m writing to. When I begin, I tell my Guardian Angel that all I want is that my letter may do some good. And, even if I only write nonsense, no one can deprive me, or my friend, of these moments spent praying for what I know he needs most."

977 "Before the letter arrived I had been feeling in low spirits, for no particular reason, and I was immensely cheered up as I read it and saw how the others are working." –And another: "Your letters and the news of my brothers help me, like a happy dream in the midst of the reality around us..." –And another: "It's so wonderful to receive those letters and to realise that I'm a friend of such friends!" –And another, and a thousand others: "I received a letter from X and am ashamed to think of my lack of spirit compared with them."

Now don't you agree that the "letter apostolate" is effective?

978 *Venite post me, et faciam vos fieri piscatores hominum* – "Come after me, and I will make you into fishers of men." –Not without reason does Our Lord use these words: men, like fish, have to be caught by the head.

What evangelical depth there is in the "apostolate of the intelligence"!

979 It's human nature to have little respect for what costs but little. –That is why I recommend to you the "apostolate of not giving".

Never fail to claim what is fairly and justly due to you from the practice of your profession, if your profession is the instrument of your apostolate.

980 "Have we not the right to take with us on our journeys a woman, a sister in Jesus Christ, to help us, as do the rest of the apostles and the brethren of the Lord and Peter himself?"

Words of Saint Paul in his first epistle to the Corinthians. –We must not disdain the cooperation of "the woman in the apostolate".

981 "And it came to pass afterwards," we read in the eighth chapter of Saint Luke, "that Jesus travelled through cities and towns, preaching and announcing the kingdom of God, and with him the twelve and certain women, who had been healed of evil spirits and sicknesses: Mary, who is called Magdalen, out of whom seven devils had been cast, and Joanna, the wife of Chusa, Herod's steward, and Susanna and others who ministered to him out of their possessions."

I copy. And I pray God that, if some woman reads me, she may be filled with a holy envy, yielding much fruit.

982 Woman is stronger than man, and more faithful, in the hour of suffering. –Mary of Magdala and Mary Cleophas and Salome!

With a group of valiant women, like these, closely united to Our Lady of Sorrows, what work of souls would be done in the world!

PERSEVERANCE

983 To begin is for everyone; to persevere, is for saints.

Let your perseverance not be a blind consequence of the first impulse, the work of inertia: let it be a reflective perseverance.

984 Say to him: *Ecce ego quia vocasti me!* –Here I am, for thou hast called me!

985 You strayed from the way, and were not coming back because you were ashamed. –It would make more sense if you were ashamed not to mend your ways.

986 "The fact is that there is no need to be in any way a hero," you confess, "to know how, without being odd or prudish, to isolate oneself as far as necessary depending on each case... and to persevere." –And you add: "So long as I carry out the norms you gave me, the scheming and gossiping in my surroundings don't worry me: to fear such trifles, that is what I would be afraid of." –Wonderful.

987 Foster and preserve that most noble ideal that has just been born within you. –Remember that many flowers blossom in the spring, and few of them grow into fruit.

988 Discouragement is an enemy of your perseverance. –If you don't fight against discouragement, you will become pessimistic, first, and lukewarm, afterwards. –Be an optimist.

989 Well, well: after so much "The Cross, Lord, the Cross!", one can see that what you wanted was a cross to your own taste.

990 Constancy, that nothing can shake. –You need it. Ask Our Lord for it and do what you can to obtain it: for it is a great safeguard against your ever parting from the fruitful way you have embarked on.

991 You cannot "rise". –It's not surprising: that fall!...

Persevere and you "will rise". –Remember what a spiritual writer has said: Your poor soul is like a bird, whose wings are still caked with mud.

Suns in heaven are needed and personal efforts, small and constant, to uproot those inclinations, those vain fancies, that depression: that mud clinging to your wings.

And you will see yourself free. –If you persevere, you "will rise".

992 Give thanks to God, who helped you, and rejoice in your victory. –What deep joy you feel in your soul, after responding!

993 You reason... well, coldly: how many motives for abandoning the task! –And some of them, seemingly, are conclusive.

I see, without doubt, that you have reasons alright. –But you are not right.

994 "My enthusiasm has gone," you

write. –You have to work not out of enthusiasm, but out of Love: conscious of duty, which means self-denial.

995 Unshakable: that is how you must be. –If your perseverance is disturbed by other people's wretchedness or by your own, I can only form a poor opinion of your ideal.

Make up your mind once and for all.

996 You have a poor idea of your way, if, when you feel cold, you think you have lost it: it is the hour of trial; that is why you have been deprived of sensible consolations.

997 Absence, isolation: trials for your perseverance. –Holy Mass, prayer, sacraments, sacrifices: Communion of Saints!: weapons to conquer with in the trial.

998 O blessed perseverance of the donkey that turns the water-wheel! –Always the same pace. Always the same circles. –One day after another: all of them the same.

Without that, there would be no ripening in the fruit, no lushness in the orchard, nor the scent of flowers in the garden.

Bring this thought to your interior life.

999 And what is the secret of perseverance? Love. –Fall in love, and you will not leave Him.

INDEX TO SCRIPTURAL REFERENCES‡

Part 1 Scripture references in *The Way*

Old Testament

‡ This index is in two parts. The first part, divided according to the books of the Old and New Testaments, includes references to Scripture in *The Way*. The second part, which follows the order of the points of *The Way,* lists references to Scripture (explicit or implicit).

New Testament

801	Luke 12:49
807	Matt 19:21-22
819	Matt 25:21.23, Luke 19:17
829	Mark 12:41-44
841	Matt 27:57-60, Mark 15:43-46, Luke 23:50-53, John 3:1ff & 19:38-42
842	Matt 5:16, 2 Cor 2:15
843	Luke 24:15-16, John 7:10, 20:14 & 21:4
872	Mark 10:13-16
879	2 Cor 11:30
904	Matt 28:19-20, Mark 16:15
906	Luke 1:33
907	Matt 10:37 Luke 2:49
912	Luke 1:38
917	Luke 24:32
921	Matt 5:13, Luke 14:34
930	Matt 7:22-23, 1 Cor 9:27
938	John 12:24
966	Mark 9:38-40
968	John 17:21
972	Ps 67:12
974	John 12:1-3
978	Mark 1:17
980	1 Cor 9:5
981	Luke 8:1-3
982	Matt 27:55-56, Mark 15:40-41, John 19:25
984	1 Sam 3:6

INDEX